# WERE THOSE THE DAYS?

# Were Those the Days?

## A VICTORIAN EDUCATION

*by*

## H. C. BARNARD

## PERGAMON PRESS

*Oxford   New York   Toronto*
*Sydney   Braunschweig*

First published by Pergamon Press Ltd.

Library of Congress Catalog Card No. 71–113359

*Printed in Great Britain by A. Wheaton & Co., Exeter*

08 007107 4

# Contents

# *Preface*

ORIGINALLY, this book was not intended for publication but was written in order that my children and grandchildren might know something of the conditions under which I was brought up and what my schooldays were like. However, it was shown to several friends who seemed to think that it might appeal to a wider circle and have "documentary value", and that it should, therefore, appear in print. Through the good offices of Dr. Edmund J. King the manuscript found its way to the Pergamon Press and was accepted by them for publication. I should like to express my sincere gratitude to Dr. King for his interest and help.

The chapter (No. 11) on John Lewis Paton is based largely on an article which I contributed to the November 1962 issue of the *British Journal of Educational Studies*. I have been enabled to use it through the kind permission of the editor, Professor A. C. F. Beales; and to him also I offer my acknowledgements and thanks. In Chapter 5, again, I have made some use of an article entitled "Victorian Private School" which I contributed to *The Times Educational Supplement* of October 7th, 1955. I should like to acknowledge the kindness of the editor in allowing me to do this.

H. C. B.

CHAPTER 1

# Introduction

OLD men are supposed to have two outstanding characteristics—
a tendency to talk about themselves and a habit of looking back,
because (as someone has cheerfully remarked) they dare not look
forward. That may explain the genesis of this book, but not the
whole of its purpose. I was born in 1884, and I went up to
Oxford in 1903. Thus the period of my childhood, youth and
adolescence coincided roughly with the last two decades of
Queen Victoria's reign, for she died in 1901. Although those days
and ours lie well within the compass of an ordinary lifetime, the
cataclysms which have occurred since the beginning of the
present century have altered existence to an extent which perhaps
can be appreciated only by those who have a clear recollection of
the Victorian world. It cannot be easy for a generation which has
spent all its life under the shadow of war, or of the effects of war,
or of military preparations on a yet more gigantic scale, to realise
the comparative simplicity of existence when I was a boy—
though it may have been a deceptive simplicity. We could read
the miserable record of evictions in Ireland, of unemployment
riots in this country, and of anarchist outrages even in London
itself. We could watch the rise of a highly organised and efficient
German Empire, and wonder what that portended for Britain.
But all these things lay outside our seemingly secure "middle-
class" existence. The continued prosperity of this country was
taken for granted, as if it were a law of nature, and there was
little to disturb the even tenor of our way.

Imagine a state of society in which there were no hydrogen bombs or cosmonauts, no aeroplanes or motor-cars, no cinemas or radio or television, no computers, no house-telephones or even electric light and power in private dwellings, no football pools or betting shops, no spy-trials or conscription (that was left to benighted foreigners), no restrictions on travel abroad. Living was cheap and prices were stable. Income-tax in 1890 was six-pence in the £; in 1899 it was raised to eightpence—and even in those days people grumbled. It was still the fashion to go to church on Sundays—at any rate in the "middle-class" society to which I belonged, though I was fortunately spared the additional burden of having to attend Sunday School, which was the fate of many children. During those last twenty years of Victoria's reign it had generally come to be believed that the British Empire had been divinely instituted in order that the remotest corners of the earth (we were doing pretty well, for example, in the scramble for Africa) might be regenerated by the missionary or exploited by the financier. There was an absolute taboo on any mention of sex. Throughout my childhood and youth no one ever gave me the slightest help in tackling the problems which are connected with this subject. The frankness—or rather, the utter lack of restraint—which characterises many of the newspapers and much of the entertainment of today, would have scandalised unspeak-ably the godly folk amongst whom I was brought up. As G. M. Trevelyan has said: "The competition of cheap journalism and literature, aimed at the lowest level of intelligence, only became dangerous at the latter end of the (nineteenth) century."* Great stress was laid on "respectability", of which "middle-class" society was the last stronghold; and one was always being admonished to behave as a "gentleman" or remember the family motto.† But with us it was, I am sure, a sincere respectability. It may have covered a narrow, puritanical outlook, and Matthew Arnold had already labelled its exponents "philistines". At any rate it was based on principle and taken seriously; and it provided a standard.

* *Ideas and Beliefs of the Victorians*, p. 18.
† "Bear and forbeare."

A "middle-class" life could be very pleasant in those days. Even the least well-to-do family could afford to keep a servant or two—a housemaid's wages were £26 a year, and a cook's £30, "all found"; and the domestic problems which paralyse modern life were to a large extent unknown. I think there is no doubt that normally domestic servants were treated with kindness and even friendliness; but the class barrier was carefully preserved. The mistress of the house was addressed and referred to as "Madam", and the children were never called by their plain Christian names, but always with the prefix "Master" or "Miss". It was also much less common then for the father of the family to do odd jobs about the house than it is now. If anything went wrong or wanted doing, a "man" was straightway sent for to cope with the situation. The amateur gardener also, I suspect, was usually of the type that wears leather gloves and limits his activities to pruning the rose bushes; and who leaves the hard digging or lawn-mowing to a hired professional. Again, it was an age in which it was possible to be quiet. The peace of the countryside when jet-planes, supersonic bangs, motor-cycles and transistors were as yet unknown, can hardly be conceived under present-day conditions. Apart from this, there was more real country available than there is today. The Germans during the last war tried to destroy our towns; but the activities of our own army and air-force (with their American associates) have contributed ever since to deprive us of more and more of our countryside. Where once there were cornfields and productive farmlands, unspoilt villages and rural beauty spots, one may now find aerodromes, bombing ranges, manoeuvering grounds for tanks, and atomic research stations. And besides all this, owing to the need for more and more houses and the increase of traffic, the inevitable urban sprawl and de-velopment of motor-ways over the open country continue and will continue.

In the late Victorian days most people certainly believed in progress, and they agreed with Herbert Spencer that this was bound up with scientific advance. That seemed to be proved by its relation to our industrial expansion and the way in which it had made possible a gradual improvement in the material conditions of life. But we little knew where all this was leading us. Scientific research can doubtless advance knowledge, but there is no guarantee that it will teach wisdom. For example, it may perhaps be debated how far the invention of the internal combustion engine has been a blessing to mankind, and the same thing may well prove to be true in regard to the discovery of nuclear energy. So our Victorian idea of progress, which has been infinitely intensified in the present technological age, may have been a deceptive one. "Progress" is still a catch-word and is commonly interpreted in reference to man's control over nature, measured in terms of power or speed. But the word literally means "taking steps forward". Just walking forward is not necessarily "progress" in the real sense. One may be walking along the primrose path to the everlasting bonfire, or the broad way that leadeth to destruction. There were thinkers even in Victorian times who realised these things—Carlyle, Ruskin and many others. Among them was Matthew Arnold who said, "To have the power of using, which is the thing wished, these data of natural science, a man must, in general, have first been *moralised*."*

The need for "moralising" scientific knowledge has been brought home to us with devastating clarity during recent years; but how the moralising may be best effected is still an unsolved problem. Matthew Arnold thought it could be achieved by means of "those old agents, letters, poetry, religion". But the Victorian intellectuals who questioned scientific "progress" seem to have been voices crying in the wilderness. The popular idea, in spite of the catastrophies of the present century, is still dominant, and has indeed developed enormously. In fact, faith in the methods and achievements of science has largely undermined what remained of our traditional Victorian beliefs and standards, which were based largely on the unquestioned authority, if not of religion, at any rate of custom. We are beginning to realise that, as a concomitant result of our material advances, there has been some moral and

* *Reports on Elementary Schools, 1852–1882*, p. 178.

spiritual regress which has reacted upon our children and adolescents and has complicated the work of education. None the less, the attempt to "moralise" scientific progress, which Matthew Arnold advocated, implies at least a knowledge of what science is. No education nowadays would leave out of account so fundamentally important an interpretation of the world around us. Yet in the last part of the Victorian era it was still possible—as I shall show from my own experience—to receive an extended education at school and the university, and yet to be given no instruction whatever in any branch of science.

A criticism of current ideas of "progress" does not imply that during the past half-century or so we have not in many respects made real advances. The most striking, perhaps, is the practical abolition of poverty. In my youth it was quite common to see children barefoot and dressed in rags. Young boys were employed to sell papers or black boots or act as scavengers or run errands. Almost every suburban street-crossing had its "sweeper"— usually a dilapidated urchin or a broken-down old man. The children of the poor showed abundant evidence of rickets and under-nourishment. Dr. Barnardo's beneficent work had been started because he discovered that hundreds of homeless boys and girls in London were sleeping under the arches and in the alleyways, since there was nowhere else for them to go. With the periodic waves of unemployment the misery increased. Gangs of men used to parade the streets singing "We've got no work to do", appealing to the charity of passers-by. I have a vivid recollection of a white-faced man and woman standing in the gutter and trying to sell two chairs from their home in order to obtain money on which to live—a case which my father investigated and found to be absolutely genuine. There was no unemployment insurance and no system of old-age pensions. For them we had to wait until the passing of Lloyd George's National Insurance Act of 1911, and The Old Age Pension Acts of 1908 and 1925. The provisions of these have been subsequently much extended. But in my youth for the aged poor there was only parish relief or the workhouse where husband and wife, in the evening of their days, were separated. The wheel has since turned full circle. The "middle-classes", who had their hey-day in those late Victorian times, are now bearing the burden and heat of the day; and the workers, whose lot was then so uncertain and often so hard, have now a measure of social security undreamt of sixty or seventy years ago. Even if it be true that the Welfare State encourages its citizens to think more often of their rights than of their duties, we should still be justified in considering the development of the social services as an illustration of "progress" in the best sense.

Of nothing is this more true than of national education. Mr. G. A. N. Lowndes has admirably demonstrated the fact in his *The Silent Social Revolution*. It was not difficult for a skilled researcher, like the author, to work out the advance which has been made in the national educational system. But in the days when I went to school this was a self-contained "elementary" system; no respectable member of a "middle-class" family, such as that to which I belonged, would dream of having anything to do with it. It was specifically designed for the children of the poor. They were herded together in enormous classes, and sometimes in most unsuitable buildings; and there they were instructed in the elements of literacy—with a few frills—largely by rote methods because of the size of the classes. One or two of the more enlightened school boards had advanced beyond this, and eventually a State system of secondary education was organised. But that was not until after 1902—i.e. outside of our "special period". Even then the distinction between the two streams—"elementary" for the poor, secondary for the rest—still remained.

A fair amount of information has become available from official and other sources as to the nature, extent and effectiveness of national education (i.e. the "elementary" system) during the last two decades of Queen Victoria's reign, and of the notable progress that has been made since; but it is perhaps more difficult to ascertain what went on in the other stream. It seemed to me, therefore, that a description of my own education between 1889 and 1903 might help to illustrate this. I cannot, of course, claim that it is *typical* of the education which a child from a "middle-class" family would receive in those days; but then no education is really "typical". Even in the mass-produced, politically conditioned education of a totalitarian country there must still be room for individual differences based on varying family conditions and general environment. Moreover, I propose to interpret the term "education" in its widest sense. Sir John Adams in his *The Evolution of Educational Theory* distinguishes "human" education and "cosmic" education. The former includes "all kinds of education in which man has deliberately taken himself in hand"; while in "cosmic" education "man's place as an educator is taken by some force that is more or less external to him".* Thus the first type would include all those planned educational influences which are exerted on the child by his school or his family or any other agency; while "cosmic" education would cover all those chance influences which may be brought to bear on him from time to time, and which, even if not designed, may none the less be powerful. Geographic environment, the traditions of the family or the group of which the child belongs, contacts with friends and companions, the interests which the child develops spontaneously, the occupations in which he chooses to engage his spare time—all these are important sources of "cosmic" education.

In this book I have not hesitated to describe my "cosmic", as well as my "human" education; because they both seem to me to illustrate an aspect of "middle-class" life in the late Victorian period, and for that reason may be worth recapturing. I have referred extensively to the background and environmental conditions of the society in which I was brought up and which ultimately had much educational significance in this "cosmic" sense. I have also endeavoured to bring out the main contrasts between this environment and that which influences or interests a child or young person in a middle-class family at the present day. This may lead to discursiveness, but I have tried to keep educational issues ultimately in view all the time. The disadvantage of drawing upon one's own experience is that it involves

* *Op. cit.*, p. 31.

an extensive use of the first personal pronoun. But, in a case like this, unless the information is at first hand the whole point is lost. It also means that one is concerned largely with what might be considered to be trivialities. But a child's life is made up of such things and they are not trivial to him; so that an adult study of a child's life must concern itself with them. With that apology and explanation, therefore, I embark upon an account of my Victorian education.

The Author, aged 4 years.

Hansom cabs in the City, about 1900 (see page 12).

The Strand with Simpsons on the right, pre-1900 (see page 13).

Little boys' costume in the 1890's. The ages of the four boys in the picture are, respectively 8,  $6\frac{1}{2}$, 3 and 2 (see page 26)

## CHAPTER 2

# London

MY FAMILY came originally from Cambridgeshire; and ultimately—so far as we have been able to trace—from the small town of Isleham, on the edge of the Fens. It afterwards lived at Barrington, a village some four miles south of Cambridge. One of my ancestors was an early member of Emmanuel College, where he took his degree in 1618.* He afterwards became vicar of a Cambridge parish and "lecturer" at St. Sepulchre's Church, London. But about the middle of the eighteenth century my branch of the family migrated to the metropolis and there became associated with the firm of manufacturing silversmiths henceforth known as Edward Barnard and Sons. It had been founded in 1680 and is now said to be the oldest firm of its kind in the country. In this way we became associated with the Goldsmiths' Company and with the City of London. My grandfather, one of my uncles, other relations and several of my ancestors further back were liverymen of the Company. I realised the appropriateness of this term when in due course I attended the sybaritic dinners given at Goldsmiths' Hall; for when I reached the age of 21 I was enabled to become a member of the Company and a freeman of the City by "patrimony"—the sixth in a direct line going back to about 1760. These matters have a purely sentimental interest and obviously imply no kind of merit; but to be a "citizen of no mean city" is perhaps as legitimate a source of pride as to have originated from the regions north of the Tweed

* See J. Venn, *Alumni Cantabrigienses*, vol. I, p. 91.

or from the largest county in England; and it is at any rate a distinction less commonly asserted. The fact remains that my family association with the City of London was a very definite element in the tradition which I inherited, and therefore in my education.

These influences were strengthened by the fact that I was born in the heart of the City itself—in King Edward Street which until 1843 had been known as Butchers' Hall Lane. It continued the direction of Little Britain southwards. Our house was destroyed by enemy action during the Second World War. If I looked out of my nursery window I could see the great dome of St. Paul's Cathedral, towering over the buildings on the other side of Newgate Street and in Paternoster Row. Close at hand was the old Christ's Hospital which covered all the area between the back of St. Bartholomew's Hospital and Newgate Street. On the west it was bounded by Giltspur Street, and on the east it extended along the whole of King Edward Street southwards from Little Britain. When the school was removed to Horsham in 1902 the buildings were pulled down and the present General Post Office was erected on the site. The school stretched as far as Christ Church, which stood at the Newgate Street corner. This was blitzed during the war, but the tower still stands. The rest of the area remains devastated; but it is being redeveloped and St. Paul's will soon be surrounded—and perhaps overtopped—by enormous boxes of concrete and glass, erected for the accommodation of typists and tycoons.

The boys of Christ's Hospital were a perennial source of interest to me. I often used to be allowed to go round to the front gates and watch them as, with their bluecoat skirts looped up and their yellow legs flashing, they kicked the ball up and down a fine open space known as "Hall-play". It was bounded on the north side by the school hall—an imposing stone building with an open cloister at its base. But even in those days central London was a curious place in which to bring up a young child. There were no public open spaces available; but as my father was friendly with the Treasurer of Christ's Hospital I was sometimes allowed to play in the garden of his house.* It was curious to find a fair-sized, suburban-type garden in the heart of the City. At other times I went into St. Paul's Churchyard to feed the pigeons, under the care of a nurse who had been for over twenty years in my father's family (he was the eldest of nine children), and who then in due course took charge of me. She was always called "Nurse", too, for the term "Nannie" had apparently not yet been invented. It was she who introduced me to the custom of saying grace, though this benediction—for some reason unknown to me—was pronounced only before breakfast and midday dinner, and never before tea or supper. Its sentiment was irreproachable, but its grammar was not beyond criticism: "For what we are about to receive may the Lord grant a blessing on."

I do not remember much about the King Edward Street house, but I have a vivid recollection of lying in bed and watching the lines of light on the ceiling, caused by the street lamp on the other side of the road sending its rays through the slats of a venetian blind. From time to time one would hear the clop-clop and jingle of a hansom cab coming down the street, and then the streaks of light would be momentarily obscured as the top of the cab and the figure of the driver passed between the lamp and the house window.

Occasionally my father would take me for an excursion. A particular delight was to ride on the top of a bus. In the 1880's an omnibus had what was called a "knifeboard" which ran longitudinally along the roof. It afforded a low and rather precarious seat for two rows of passengers who sat back to back. To climb the ladder which led to this eminence required some acrobatic agility, and the "knifeboard" was therefore reserved for young and active members of the male sex. But there were also one or two privileged seats on each side of the driver, facing the horse(s). There one had a kaleidoscopic vista of the road in front, and even the distinction of conversation with the driver himself.

In those days, of course, the streets of London presented a

* There is a picture of this in E. H. Pearce, *Annals of Christ's Hospital*, p. 294.

very different picture from that of the present. There were numerous horse-buses, holding perhaps twenty passengers inside and twelve or fourteen on the "knifeboard", with the conductor hanging on precariously just outside the door. They were of many different colours and patterns, because they belonged to different companies which competed for passengers. They had no fixed stopping-places, and one normally hailed them as one hails a taxi-cab nowadays. Travelling by bus was regarded—at any rate in my stratum of society—as a rather plebeian form of transport; and the more fashionable vehicle was the hansom cab —"the gondola of London". It had only two wheels and took two passengers who faced towards the front. The driver sat up high behind, and the reins came down over the roof and onto the horse's back. There was an ingenious contraption of doors which folded back in front of the wheels. Once the fare was safely inside the doors were shut, although one could easily see over the top of them. This mechanism, which could be worked by the driver, was a source of much interest to a small boy. Another intriguing arrangement was a little trap-door at the back of the roof of the cab through which one could hold a conversation with the driver. Altogether a ride in a hansom was a thrilling experience.

For humbler folk, or for travellers with luggage, the more ordinary means of conveyance was the "growler", or four-wheeled cab. Whereas the driver of a hansom usually affected a rather dashing and "horsey" get-up, as if he were going to the Races, the "growler" cabman was more often of the "jarvie" type, with less care for his appearance.

Most of the streets were macadamised, but some were paved with stones rather like the granite "sets" which are still found in some of the big manufacturing towns of northern England. But the use of asphalt for paving purposes was already becoming common. This led to a good many protests, because it was feared that the smooth surface, especially in wet weather, might result in horses slipping down—particularly in the case of hansom cabs; this did, in fact, happen from time to time. Another improvement was the introduction of hard wood blocks. For this purpose two

Australian trees—jarrah and kauri—were chiefly used and they had the advantage of making for quietness and being less likely to cause horses to slip.

Owing to the large number of buses and cabs and drays and horse-drawn vehicles of all kinds, there was already a London traffic problem. There was also apparently little systematic attempt to deal with it, though occasionally a policeman would do his best to stem the stream and shepherd pedestrians across. As a rule if one wanted to cross the street one just dashed to a refuge in the middle of the road when an opportunity offered, and then waited for another chance to reach the other side. The visitor from the country found these experiences somewhat hair-raising; but it was of no use to wait for the stream to stop, for there were no traffic lights—*Rusticus expectat dum defluat amnis.*

In the midst of all this turmoil white-coated men and boys, armed with a brush in one hand and a kind of dust-pan in the other, used to dash in and out of the traffic at the very peril of their lives, scooping up the horse-droppings with which the streets were continually being fouled. This ordure was tipped into iron bins, four or five feet high and open at the top, which stood at intervals along the edge of the pavement. These were periodically emptied with shovels into a scavenger's cart—surely a most unhygienic arrangement.

But sometimes the scene would suddenly change. In the distance a shout of "Hi! Hi!" and the clatter of hoofs could be heard, coming nearer and nearer. The police would dash into the road and hold up all the traffic so as to clear an avenue—and then a glorious sight: the fire-engine with galloping horses and a group of firemen with flashing helmets perched precariously along the top. Beside the driver sat a man whose continued shouting gave the warning for clearing the way; and at the back was the gleaming brass-covered boiler of the pumping-engine, from the funnel of which poured smoke and steam and even real flames. The most up-to-date motor fire-engine can never furnish a thrill like that. No wonder that all the boys and young men started running to see where the fire was and to watch the fun.

The London Fire Brigade was indeed a most popular institution and the head of it, Captain Shaw, was a national figure. He is immortalised in Gilbert and Sullivan's *Iolanthe*—

> O Captain Shaw!
> Type of true love kept under,
> Could thy Brigade
> With cool cascade
> Quench my great love, I wonder!

Shaw was Chief Officer of the London Fire Brigade for thirty years, from 1861 to 1891, and when he retired he was given the K.C.B. and became Sir Eyre Maney Shaw.

The almost universal street illuminant in London, when I lived there, was gas. A "lamplighter" used to go round with a long pole on the top of which was a perforated metal case containing a lighted torch. As he came to each lamp-post he pushed up the tap, and the gas ignited. The jet itself was protected by a four-sided glass shade, larger at the top than at the bottom. Sometimes a slip of dark-blue glass, on which the street name was etched in white, was inserted along one side of the shade; so that at night it was easy to recognise one's whereabouts. Electric light was practically unknown. I first saw it in the form of huge, globular, dazzling-white arc lamps, used to illuminate a railway marshalling yard. But even the gas lamps were powerless against a London fog. The "pea-souper" of my early youth is, I think, practically extinct, although the London fog problem remains a serious one. Traffic perforce came practically to a standstill and pedestrians groped their way about, often with the assistance of link-boys or youths carrying flares. The police had their bull's-eye lanterns which were, of course, part of their regular equipment and were attached to their belts.

So there was always something of interest in my walks abroad, although my memory of London of nearly eighty years ago is inevitably faint and fragmentary. But another excursion to which I greatly looked forward was a visit to the "works" in Angel Street. The ancestral firm not only made silver articles like spoons and forks, teasets and napkin-rings, but it also specialised on such works of art as presentation cups and salvers, regimental trophies and maces for colonial governments. There were two or three artists on the premises who spent their whole time in designing these masterpieces of silverware. The actual craftwork was done mainly by hand. With the exception of a rolling mill, through which the sheets of silver were put like washing through a mangle, and a few buffing-wheels for polishing, there was little machinery. Many of the employees had spent their whole lives in the service of the firm. They had entered as boys and had been apprenticed. At the end of seven years they obtained their membership of the Goldsmiths' Company and the freedom of the City by "servitude"—just as I in due course qualified for mine by "patrimony". It was a survival of the old guild system. It implied that the master should take a personal interest in his apprentices, who in the old days lived with him and his family. When I was admitted to membership of the Goldsmiths' Company there was put into my hands a book called *Rules for the Conduct of Life, to which are added a few Cautions for the use of such Freemen of London as take Apprentices.* It contained a number of didactic maxims and quotations from the Scriptures; and I was admonished to make use of it in the instruction of my apprentices. Something of this old personal interest in the workers on the part of the employer still remained in our firm. Many of the older craftsmen had known my father when he was a small boy; and he often used to recall how once, when he was taking me round the factory, one of the workmen exclaimed "Law, Sir, that your son? Why, it's scarcely creditable!" The men sat at benches, covered with leather, on which their work was put. There it was cut and carved and chased and hammered with the utmost art. I well remember seeing a silver cavalry drum, of the "timpani" type, in course of manufacture. It was the simplest, and yet the most skilful, of operations. A circular sheet of silver, 5 or 6 feet in diameter, was taken; and it was hammered and hammered and hammered for weeks on end until it had assumed a cup-like shape, and had acquired a timbre which no mechanical process could have produced.

My grandfather, who was the head of the firm, lived at Canonbury House, only 2 miles from King Edward Street, but in those days in a not unfashionable residential area. I was frequently taken to stay there. The house was surrounded by a garden which was well below the level of the adjacent streets and was protected by a high wall. In this wall there was a door, and when one rang the bell a maid would pull a lever in the kitchen. This was connected with the latch by a wire, so that with a click the door suddenly became ajar. This again was a very intriguing apparatus for a small boy. When one pushed the door open and entered one found oneself at the top of a flight of stone steps which led down to the level of the garden, through which a flagged path stretched onwards to the front door of the house. Sometimes I used to go out when the "organ-man" visited us. He was allowed to come inside the street door and to stand at the top of the steps while he gave his performance. He had a box-shaped organ on a stick. It contained a set of pipes, and turning the handle not only controlled their mechanism but also supplied the necessary wind. Many "organ-men" of this type were accompanied by a monkey who sat on the top of the box soliciting alms while the performance was being given, and on the owner's shoulder when he was trudging through the streets. At the time of which I am writing this box-shaped hand organ was giving place to the street-piano, which was mounted on wheels and contained strings with hammers operated by a barrel fitted with pins. No gradation of tone was possible, but all the popular airs, embellished with a continual stream of cheerful notes, were in the repertoire. Even the street-piano now seems to be practically obsolete.

Canonbury House itself had a considerable historical interest.* Originally there was here a house belonging to the Priory of St. Bartholomew, Smithfield, which was close to my birthplace. It was rebuilt early in the sixteenth century by a prior named

---

* It is fully described with plans and illustrations in the Royal Commission on Historical Monuments volume *London West*, pp. 64–67 and plates 101, 102 and 103. The house, alas, was demolished in 1964.

William Bolton. His rebus (a bolt in a tun) was carved in several places on the garden wall. As time went on parts of the original house were pulled down and other parts were added; but by the latter part of the nineteenth century an L-shaped building remained—some of it over 300 years old. This was divided into two dwelling-houses; the eastern "range" was that in which my grandfather lived, while the southern "range" was occupied by another family who had a boy of my own age named "Seppy" (?Septimus). The whole house was full of interesting features—notably the carved fire-places and the plaster-work of the ceilings. One of the latter showed a number of medallion busts of classical worthies; but the one which I remember best included a beautiful Tudor warship in full sail, which took one back to the days of the Armada.*

In spite of its size and its various amenities Canonbury House did not possess a bathroom. When I went to stay there one of my aunts would give me my bath in a circular tub supplied with hot water which had been brought up in cans from the kitchen by one of the maids. I suspect that it was not at all unusual for the older dwelling-houses in my young days to be unprovided with a bathroom. A contraption sometimes used consisted of a sort of water-proof tent over a saucer-shaped bath; and on the top of this was a small tank. One got inside the tent, and standing in the bath pulled a rope. The result was a shower, hot or cold according to the temperature of the water which had been put into the tank.

The actual building of Canonbury House had originally comprised a west "range" also, so that it had enclosed a courtyard on three sides of a square. The garden of our house occupied part of the site of this courtyard. But on the northern end of the west "range" was Canonbury Tower, which still exists. Like the rest of the original building, it had been extensively altered and obscured by subsequent additions; but the Tower stands up clearly in the centre and contains some exceedingly beautiful panelled rooms. The Tower is reputed to have been used by

* It is illustrated in *London West* plate 103.

Queen Elizabeth as a hunting-box, and it has also literary associations. Oliver Goldsmith, for example, resided here at the time when he wrote *The Deserted Village* and part of *The Vicar of Wakefield*.

My actual residence in London came to an end before I was 5, though I still often went to Canonbury and I have ever since been a very frequent visitor to my native city. I can never feel that it is just a huge conglomeration of buildings with no individuality or personality—still less that it is a "wen", or that Shelley was justified when he compared it to that other smoky and populous city—Hell. Even if the City is no longer a residential area, it is still soaked in history which goes back to Roman times, and even before that. It maintains unimpaired its proud traditions and ancient customs. But to me it will always be my first home—a friendly place. I can say, as did the Scotsman William Dunbar more than 400 years ago,

> London, thou art the flower of cities all,
> Gemme of all joy, jasper of jocunditie;

or more intimately, I can echo the words of my fellow-Cockney, Edmund Spenser:

> Merry London, my most kindly nurse,
> That gave to me this life's first native source.

## CHAPTER 3

# *Thornton Heath*

THE air of a great city is not always salubrious, and my mother's health in the early years of her married life had already begun to break down. Thus it happened that before I had reached the age of 5 we left the house in King Edward Street and went to live with my maternal grandfather who had recently become a widower. What a change from the heart of London! He lived at Thornton Heath near Croydon—a village which had largely lost its original character and was in process of being converted into a suburb. His house stood in the London Road, near the pond, and it had a large garden, every nook and cranny of which I soon got to know. Even today I could draw a detailed plan of it, marking in the tennis lawn, the flower garden, the shrubberies, and showing the position of the various fruit trees and vegetables. There was a large greenhouse in which my grandfather used to grow melons with a kind of mesh-pattern on their rinds, and with a pinkish interior which smelt like hair-oil. There were also some stables containing a "barouche". When a horse was needed one was hired from a neighbouring "livery and bait" establishment. In one corner of the stable yard there was a rubbish bunker, made of wood, into which all the household refuse was thrown. This was dug out from time to time by the dustmen, through a trap-door outside at ground level; and it was carried in filthy baskets out to the cart in the road. A more insanitary way of dealing with refuse could hardly have been devised.

The house itself was pleasant and commodious; and it was a shock to me many years later, when I was returning from the south coast along the London Road through Thornton Heath, to find that my old home had been pulled down, and that an enormous cinema had been erected on its site. The whole area has, of course, changed utterly in the last seventy years. When as a small boy I stood on the rubbish heap at the bottom of the garden I could look over the wall on to open country stretching away towards Mitcham Common, and to the lavender fields from which, when the wind was in the right direction, a delightful scent was wafted. A few other houses had been built along the road towards Norbury; but beyond them there were still some woods before the houses began again near Norbury station. The pond, just along the road in the other direction, had a kind of ford at one side, and carters used to drive their horses through the water to clean and refresh their feet. In the centre of the pond was a fountain which had been erected as a belated memorial of Queen Victoria's first Jubilee.

Thornton Heath was an entertaining place in which to live. The garden lent itself to endless games of exploration, though one had to beware of getting on the wrong side of the gardener who was not inappropriately named Sylvester, and who lived in a flat over the stables. From time to time there were drives round the open country in the "barouche" towards Hackbridge or Carshalton or Wallington or other places which were still villages. Sometimes we would have a picnic to Croham Hurst, an upland not far beyond Croydon. Another adventure was to be given a ride by the grocer's delivery man. He had a light vehicle, rather like a dog-cart, in which he came from Pelton's shop in Croydon; and he would sometimes take me with him on his rounds down the road and bring me back on his return journey. Occasionally one could even watch the coach go past. It was the smart thing in those days for young men of wealth and fashion to drive down to the Epsom races in a four-in-hand of the old style. This equipage presented a fine sight with its high-stepping horses, its top-hatted aristocrats, and perhaps a bevy of fine ladies as well. One has to turn to the pages of contemporary *Punch* to recapture that scene.

My grandfather's domestic staff consisted of a cook, two housemaids (of whom the senior, named Ellen, was a great friend of mine), and a butler called Salmon. The kitchen was normally out of bounds to me, but from time to time the cook, who was a motherly soul, would permit me to visit it, and then I was usually regaled with a jam-tart or a piece of cake. I was always particularly intrigued by the apparatus for roasting meat. The operation was performed in front of the open fire in the kitchen grate. A sort of oven, open on the side facing the fire and with a dripping pan at the base, was used. It was technically known as a "meat screen". The joint was suspended from the top and above it was a contrivance called a "jack". This was operated by clock-work and it ensured that the meat hanging underneath would slowly revolve throughout the process of cooking until it was completely "done" on all sides. The juices were collected in the dripping pan below. I used somehow to associate this term "done" with the phrase "Thy will be done" in the Lord's Prayer, and it caused me a good deal of perplexity. It sounded as if it ought to be "Thou wilt be done", but even that did not make sense. I have often thought that this illustrates the dangers of premature religious instruction in the case of young children. We have all heard of the little boy who said "God's name's the same as mine isn't it?"—explained by reference to the phrase "Harold be thy name". My own daughter many years later once said to her mother "God's a fish, isn't he?" and even when she was already a schoolgirl she was heard singing "For all the saints who from their neighbours rest".

To return to matters domestic: in one corner of the scullery, which adjoined the kitchen in the Thornton Heath house, stood the copper. This was a contrivance built of brick and containing a large metal receptacle underneath which there was a fireplace. The copper had to be filled with water and the fire lighted. At an appropriate moment the dirty clothes and a suitable amount of soap were inserted—the large variety of detergents available today had not yet been invented. Then a wooden lid was put on and the contents boiled. After this the clothes had to be extracted with the aid of a "copper stick" and put in the sink to drain. In order to empty the copper it had to be baled out by hand. The next process was to squeeze out the remaining moisture in the clothes by means of a mangle. This machine consisted of two wooden rollers operated by a hand-wheel, and the water ran out on to a draining-board and thence into a tub located below in order to receive it. After that, of course, everything had to be hung out to dry and finally ironed. There were no electric irons in those days, but cast iron "flat irons" were used and these had to be heated up on the kitchen stove. What a performance! The modern housewife would probably put the dirty clothes into a washing-machine or take them in the back of the car to the nearest "launderette" or "washeteria", and leave them there while she went off to the neighbouring supermarket in order to do the shopping.

The two housemaids always wore "uniform"—a print dress in the morning and a black dress with a white cap and apron in the afternoon and evening. One of Ellen's duties was to go upstairs in the early evening and light the gas-lamps on the landings and in the bedrooms. The flame was turned down to a mere bead of light but it was easy to turn it up when necessary—just as easy as switching on a modern electric light, In the winter time Ellen also had the duty of lighting the fires in the bedrooms. This must have involved a good deal of work, because the ashes would have to be removed in the morning and the fire relaid. But in those days central heating in private houses was unknown and radiators or similar contrivances in bedrooms—except occasionally cumbrous oil-stoves—were unknown. These facts illustrate the large part which the supply of domestic labour played in the life of the middle-class family in the days of my childhood. The development of labour-saving appliances of many kinds has been one of the most striking features of recent times.

The butler, Salmon, spent most of his time in a small pantry opposite the top of the cellar stairs, but I did not have much to do with him and am not sure what he did there. He used to wait at table. The second housemaid distinguished herself one day by falling through a skylight situated over the central well of the house, and she bounced on the staircase amid a shower of broken glass. She had been sent up to the loft where the skylight was and in the process of cleaning it had inadvertently trodden on one of the panes. She was hurried off to hospital and not replaced; but instead we had a daily girl. She possessed the very unusual christian name of Prin. Many years later my father told me that when she applied for the job she presented a "reference" (the term usually applied was "a character") in which her name was spelt "Phryne". How she came by such an appellation remained a mystery. It is to be hoped that it was inappropriate as regards her moral character, and it certainly did not befit her as regards personal appearance.

Prin used to help with washing-up, preparing vegetables and made herself generally useful. She also had the job of cleaning the boots. The blacking was not supplied in the neat little tins which are used nowadays but in earthenware jars provided by a firm called Day and Martin. These contained a black compound which had to be diluted with water and was daubed on to the boots with the aid of a piece of stick. It was then smeared over the leather with one brush and polished with another. In those days the custom of wearing shoes out of doors was not at all prevalent. Women wore button boots which had to be done up with an implement called a button-hook. Men usually had laced boots with little hooks to expedite the process of doing them up. I remember when I was in my 'teens going with my father to a school prize-giving at which he was the chief performer and therefore had to sit at the front of the platform in full view of the audience. When he was called upon to make his speech he writhed and was unable at first to stand up. The reason was that while sitting down he had crossed his feet and the laces of one boot had become hitched up in the hooks of the other.

To return for a moment to Prin—she was responsible for cleaning the knives. They were of the steel variety because stainless knives were unknown. These were not invented until 1913. The cleaning was done on a knife-board worked on the same principle as a razor strop, but it had first of all to be sprinkled with a special powder. It was a little later on—about the turn of the century—that I made the acquaintance of knife-cleaning machines which had been introduced by a firm called Kent.

All these domestic processes and arrangements interested me vastly because I had never had any contact with them in our King Edward Street house, and anyway I was probably too young then to take notice of them. But it has often struck me since that in those late Victorian days, in spite of the aid afforded by domestic servants, housekeeping must have been a much more complicated business than it is today. The modern housewife relies to so large an extent on comestibles supplied in packets and tins, but I think such things were much less common in my childhood. The huge joints of meat which I used to see revolving in front of the kitchen fire would be impossibly expensive for the average modern household. I have visions of large blocks of ribs of beef served up on a huge dish which had a sort of river-system entrenched in it. There was a main stream, with tributaries, down the middle, and this led into a small lake at one end of the dish where the juices from the meat were collected. The joint was served with stag-horn handled carvers of gigantic proportions— I still possess them; and there was always a preliminary sharpening display with the aid of an implement called a steel. I wonder if this is still a standard practice in the average home.

Another matter in this connection which strikes me—if a mere man may venture to discuss housekeeping matters—is that it must have been very difficult in my young days to keep food fresh for any length of time. There were, of course, no gas or electric refrigerators. Our cellar at Thornton Heath was certainly a cool place with stone shelves, and Salmon used to keep his wine-bins there. But temperatures low enough to reach freezing point were obviously impossible. In the fishmongers' shops the articles for sale were laid out on ice, and I suppose something similar was done by butchers. From time to time one would see a cart being drawn through the streets and carrying a large block of ice covered with a piece of sacking. According to a copy of *Mrs. Beeton's Cookery Book* published in the 1880's, large quantities of ice for use in fishmongers' and butchers' shops were imported from Norway. All the same, in both kinds of establishment it was common in summer to see the fish or meat covered with flies and bluebottles, a state of affairs which since those days has fortunately been remedied. Some private establishments even possessed an ice-house in which a supply of the commodity could be kept. Ices and ice-puddings could be made at home in an ice-chest supplied with a block of ice, or in a contrivance called an ice-pot. This had a smaller container inside a larger one. The comestible was put into the inner receptacle, and the space between it and the outer one was filled with ice and salt. This had the effect of refrigerating the contents.

My nursery was on the first floor of our Thornton Heath house, overlooking the stable yard where Sylvester, the gardener, washed down the "barouche". To watch him doing this was an unfailing source of interest, and it was understood that due notice was to be given to me when the operation was to be carried out. But though I had my meals (or some of them) in the nursery it was not altogether a play-room. It contained a rocking-horse; but, as far as I can remember, I had far fewer toys than most children seem to have nowadays. The stage of leaden soldiers and model trains came later, but I was fond of using chalk and paints. Sometimes the nursery would be commandeered for the visit of the "needle-woman". She came for the whole day and stayed to dinner which she had in my room. She used to tell me tales of her lodger who played the euphonium in the Salvation Army band. One of his most thrilling exploits, which excited my deep admiration, was to kill a mouse by holding the mouth of his instrument over the top of the trap in which the victim was, and then blowing a tremendous blast—a veritable trump of doom. The needle-woman did all the mending and alterations and adjustments which had accumulated since her last visit. She even made dresses. We possessed a wire contraption, resembling in outline the female frame, on which garments were fitted while these operations were being carried out. This machine was known in the family as "Miss Brown". But ours was no ordinary Miss Brown. By turning a handle near the base she could be made to expand or contract, so that at one time she might meet the requirements of a buxom matron of middle-age, and then be manipulated so as to counterfeit the slimness and *sveltesse* of a ballerina. "Miss Brown" was a perennial source of interest and delight to me. I never tired of turning the handle and putting her through her evolutions.

It was not only the female members of the household who benefited by the needle-woman's ministrations. Sometimes I too would be brought in to have a blouse fitted or a pair of knickers tried on. The usual costume for small boys in those days was a comfortable and informal sailor suit made of dark-blue serge. But on Sundays we had to toe the line. One wore a similar suit, usually white or striped, with a rather stiff light-blue collar on which there were lines of white braid. Under this a black silk scarf was tied and knotted in front; and to it was added a lanyard, with a whistle tucked into a breast pocket. One was, in fact, a replica of a naval rating, in full dress, except that knickers were substituted for bell-bottomed trousers. On one's head one wore an ordinary sailor's cap, complete with ribbon showing the name of some well-known warship. In summer this was replaced by a wide-brimmed nautical hat made of pliant straw, and secured by an uncomfortable piece of elastic under the chin. When this began to get loose a knot was tied in it; and that made it even more uncomfortable. All the same, sailor suits were a sensible dress for a small boy, and if one were lucky one might be allowed sometimes to wear a jersey. Of course, some fond mothers fitted out their offspring with more elaborate costumes. One unfortunate urchin at my kindergarten school used to appear in a kilt, and became an object of derision to the other little boys. I myself, on one occasion, was detailed to act as a page at the wedding of my uncle. I was dressed up in a little Lord Fauntleroy costume of green velvet, with a deep lace collar, and globular brass buttons; but to my great relief this was the only time, so far as I can remember, that I was required to appear in this guise.

CHAPTER 4

# *Early Lessons*

THE state of my mother's health made it necessary for her to spend most of her time at various resorts, and she was rarely at home. My father also was often away. This meant that after my family nurse was pensioned off I was left for the most part in the care of various governesses, some of whom I loved and some of whom I hated. Praised be the buxom Amy Franklin who mothered a rather lonely little boy! Once when we were on holiday by the seaside it became necessary for me to sleep in her bed; and at breakfast next morning (so I am told) I caused her some embarrassment, and the rest of the company some amusement, by exclaiming "I do like sleeping with Miss Franklin. She's so fat and comfortable!" But unfortunately she was succeeded by a Miss Spong, a pruney and prismatic lady of Anglo-Catholic (or, as the term went in those days, "ritualistic") tendencies. On one occasion she sent me to bed for having poured some furniture polish on the stair carpet (after having first tasted it to see what it was like). I can even yet remember the joy with which, in retaliation, I put a large prayer-book, to which she was inordinately attached, into a can of water in the bathroom. She confronted me with the dripping object and said in a cold and forbidding voice "I wonder who did this?" To which I ingenuously replied "I wonder?"

My maternal grandfather took a great interest in public affairs. He was among the first aldermen of Croydon when this town was granted the status of a borough. But he was also appointed Deputy-Chairman of the London County Council when this was formed in 1889. His activities brought him into contact with some of the notables of the time, and occasionally they would find their way to Thornton Heath; and then I would be sent for and exhibited. In particular, my grandfather used to give an annual dinner to which his official friends were invited. I remember, for example, the boyish-looking Lord Rosebery who was Chairman of the L.C.C., and with whom of course my grandfather had close contact. I had to retire to bed when the butler, Salmon, announced "Dinner is served". But a little later a plate containing a slice of pineapple would be brought to me with Lord Rosebery's compliments and a request that I would "draw an engine" for him. Another visitor was Sir John Lubbock, who became Lord Avebury. He was a scholar and a scientist of extraordinary versatility, as well as a banker and a man of affairs; but he was also not above talking to a child on matters which might interest him. He used to tell me about the experiments which he was performing with his ants. However, it was rather confusing for a small boy, because he always pronounced the word "aunts". Yet another visitor of a very different type was John Burns. He was greatly admired by my grandfather who was, for those days, an advanced liberal. John Burns was a working-man who had educated himself, and taken to politics; he was in fact an early example of a type which the Labour Party has since made familiar. He had even spent some time in prison on a charge of inciting the Trafalgar Square unemployment riots of 1886. He had been elected to the L.C.C. as progressive member for Battersea, and it was thus that my grandfather got to know him. He subsequently entered Parliament and was made President of the Board of Trade in Sir Henry Campbell-Bannerman's administration. He was the first working-man to attain Cabinet rank. Another frequent visitor to our house was a neighbour named Hobbs, who was a fellow-alderman of Croydon with my grandfather. Some time after the latter's death we were shocked to learn that our former friend had been concerned, together with another financier named Jabez Balfour, in a series of extensive frauds associated with the Liberator Building Society.* As the result of their speculations large numbers of poor people had lost all their savings, and the affair created a great scandal at the time. Balfour sought to avoid being brought to justice by fleeing to South America; but he was extradited and taken back to this country. Both he and Hobbs were committed to Wormwood Scrubbs for a long term of imprisonment.

From time to time we went on holiday to the seaside—sometimes to the particular resort where my mother was vainly trying to recover her health. Today such an excursion implies little more than putting some luggage into the boot of the car and driving off to one's destination. But with my grandfather a seaside holiday involved a considerable amount of organisation. We often combined with a family of cousins who also lived in Thornton Heath. In the first place a whole furnished house was usually hired for a month or so, and a couple of servants were sent in advance to get it ready. When the day of departure arrived a railway omnibus took us and our luggage to Victoria or some other London terminus. As we drew near the station one or two street loafers would run alongside the bus in the hope of earning a shilling by helping to unload the baggage. There were, of course, no corridor carriages on the trains in those days, but we travelled in a reserved compartment. The venue was usually one of the south-coast resorts—Whitstable, Folkestone, Hastings, Eastbourne—Sandown or Ventnor in the Isle of Wight. When we returned the same routine was observed.

As we simply changed houses and took our own domestic staff with us a seaside holiday was not essentially very different from life at home. We certainly went out more for drives in a hired carriage, and it was always pleasant to play on the beach. The chief holiday attraction was bathing. Those were the days of bathing-machines—sheds mounted on four wheels and hauled up and down at the edge of the sea by a horse with a man on his back. Each machine had either one or two damp and sandy compartments in which the bathers undressed. This done, the

* See *Encyclopaedia Britannica* (11th edition), vol. IV, p. 768.

contraption was jolted down into the water, and one descended by means of some steps at the back. There were set hours of male and female bathing, and mixed bathing was strictly taboo. In spite of my sex, however, and as a privilege due to my extreme youth, I was permitted to bathe with either the masculine or the feminine members of my family—whichever happened to be the more convenient. I preferred to accompany my father, for then I could jump off the steps into the water and pretend to be a frog, or could ride on his back while he was swimming. It was apparently considered unladylike to be able to swim, and female bathers usually contented themselves with bobbing up and down while holding on to a rope at the back of the bathing machine, while I was left to the ministrations of a "bathing woman" who had a habit of ducking her charges head under without any of the fun of diving.

In my childhood the custom of taking seaside holidays had become general even among the poorer classes. Excursion trains brought crowds of "trippers" to watering-places like Margate, Ramsgate, Brighton or Blackpool. There they were entertained on the sands by nigger minstrels or by a Punch and Judy show and regaled by the sellers of cockles and winkles who trundled their barrows around. As a contrast to these dissipations outdoor religious services, designed mainly for children, were often held on the beach. A couple of earnest evangelists would conduct the proceedings, and hymns were sung to the accompaniment of a portable harmonium played by a devoted young lady. I wonder if these practices still persist. But it was not only the seaside resorts that were invaded by the masses from London. There was an annual exodus from the East End to the hop fields of Kent. The hop-picking was all done by hand and work was found for everyone, including the children. The "hoppers" were often accommodated in special living quarters which had been erected by their employers. The hops were afterwards dried in the oast houses which still form so picturesque a feature of the Kentish countryside.

I received my earliest lessons from the governesses to whom I have already referred. It was from them that I learnt to read, and they must have been effective teachers because I early became fairly proficient in this art. As a result I was able to profit, more or less unaided, by what nowadays is called "silent reading", and for an only child, whose mother was an invalid and who was left a good deal to his own devices, this was a great advantage. I was never tired of the "Alice" books, with their delightful Tenniel illustrations; in fact I could soon quote large passages from them by heart. They were indeed a "possession for ever", for at any period of life they have always some fresh charm for the reader. Even now I can get almost as much pleasure from remaking their acquaintance as when, at the age of 6 or 7, I lay on the hearthrug in the drawing-room and made my first exploration of Wonderland and the Looking-Glass country. Another constant source of interest was some bound volumes of *Good Words for the Young*, which had come from my father's family. This magazine had existed from 1869 to 1872 and, in spite of its rather forbidding title, it formed a refreshing contrast to the highly didactic type of periodical literature which had hitherto been considered suitable for children. Many of its articles and stories were illustrated with delightful woodcuts. It was through this magazine that I became acquainted with George Macdonald's *The Princess and the Goblin* and *At the back of the North Wind*, which are surely classics of children's literature. Other stories which appeared for the first time in *Good Words for the Young* were Charles Kingsley's *Madam How and Lady Why*, Henry Kingsley's *The Boy in Grey*, and Gilbert à Beckett's *King George's Middy*. There was something for children of all ages. As a contrast to this I was never tired of looking at a volume entitled *Discoveries and Inventions of the Nineteenth Century*. This entrancing tome contained illustrations of trains crossing the prairies of central North America, an account of the *Great Eastern*, a section of a steam locomotive, and a picture of one of the old broad-gauge engines the boiler of which had exploded. A good deal of attention was given to such subjects as battleships, naval guns and torpedoes. There was even an illustration of the very fire-engine (made by Merryweather) which I had seen in the streets of London.

The fact that I had already learnt to read and had acquired the habit of "browsing" at home was a help to me when I first started to go to school. It was situated at some distance from our house, on the other side of Thornton Heath station. I came to be taken there by the upper housemaid, Ellen, and she came to fetch me again in the afternoon. We used to make the most of the journey by tram. Like the contemporary omnibuses, it had two rows of seats inside, facing one another. On top, however, was a series of seats with a central gangway. They were exposed to the weather, but a tarpaulin apron was often provided to put over one's lap and legs if it rained. The tram was drawn by horses—two of them, as a rule; but for a short time on our tram-line steam locomotives were used and I believe that this method of traction was used quite extensively in some of the big industrial towns. Another ingenious device was the cable system. In this case a narrow continuous slot between the tram-lines gave access to an underground conduit along which an endless cable passed. This was kept in continual motion by a steam-engine in a power house. The tram was provided with an apparatus which reached down through the slot and gripped the cable which thus provided the necessary motive power. It was a method used particularly where trams had to ascend steep gradients. There was a cable tramway, for example, up Highgate Hill in north London. Electric traction was a rather later stage of development, but any form of tramway now seems practically obsolete. The system had its disadvantages. The existence of the grooved rails on the surface of the road and the granite sets in which they were fixed engendered difficulties for other types of traffic—especially for bicycles which were liable to get their tyres entangled in the tram-lines. The slot of the cable tramway was a particular nuisance. Also it was not easy to pass a tram which was confined to a track in the middle of the road. It was certainly allowable to overhaul it on the near side, but one had to avoid carefully the passengers who were getting on or off at a stopping-place.

Queuing up in an orderly fashion did not become a standard
practice until the time of the First World War. Before that the
crowd of waiting passengers just surged forward in a mass as
soon as the tram arrived. The disappearance of the tram may
legitimately be regarded as a sign of progress, and the motor-bus
which is not confined to a prescribed track and can move more
freely about the road certainly has advantages. One is reminded
of Ronald Knox's limerick about the undergraduate who was
studying the problem of predestination and free-will—

> There was a young man who said "Damn!
> At last I've found out that I am
>     A creature that moves
>     In determinate grooves—
> In fact, not a bus, but a tram!"

I return from this long digression to describe my first school
at which I have now arrived by means of the tram. It called itself
a "kindergarten".

Since the middle of the nineteenth century the educational
theories of Froebel had excited a good deal of interest in this
country, and various associations and committees had been
formed to foster them and put them into practice. The Froebel
Society itself dates from about 1875, and the work of training
kindergarten teachers was begun. It is probable that many private
schools for young children came into existence, which were not
staffed by officially trained and qualified Froebel teachers and
which did not adopt with any precision the particular techniques
of Froebelianism. But they called themselves "kindergartens",
and they did stand for encouraging the child to be active, to
express himself in speech and song and movement, and to be
intelligently interested in his environment. In an age when
classes in the primary schools, sponsored by the school boards
or the Church, contained fifty or sixty or even more pupils,
taught by rote methods and under iron discipline, the kindergartens dealt with children in small groups so that individual
requirements could be studied and catered for. At the same time
they were not treated as research fodder for aspiring educational

Ph.D.s or made the subject of elaborate questionnaires and psychological investigations.

The particular kindergarten of which I became a member was a school of this type. It was probably the best school that I ever attended, and the modern infant school, with its "activities" and "centres of interest", had little to teach it in the way of techniques. We paraded to the strains of Hill's *March in D*, played skilfully on an excellent piano by a mistress one of whose eyes was blue and the other brown. We danced and mimed; we learnt a whole repertoire of hymns and songs appropriate to our age. How well I remember:

> Here we float in a golden boat
> Far away, far away . . .

—as we sat in a line on the floor, pulling rhythmically at our imaginary oars, while the steersman, facing us at the stern, carried the flag. We even produced a play—*The Maid and the Blackbird*. In this I took the part of the King and had to sing a solo. Sand and modelling clay played a large part in our manual activities, and we also plaited strips of shiny coloured paper into patterns. On one occasion we constructed on the floor of the schoolroom a plan of the neighbourhood, using oblong wooden blocks to indicate the roads and showing the houses where the various pupils lived by means of the square boxes in which the blocks were kept. It was in this school that I received my first prize—an individual present from a motherly teacher for whom I had a great affection. It took the form of a copy of *Mary's Meadow*, by Juliana Horatia Ewing; and it introduced me to the other works of that delightful authoress. Another of my kindergarten teachers was a lady with a mop of hair (like Mrs. Cimabue Brown's in Du Maurier's drawings), and a willowy form, encased in a tight-fitting bluey-green velvet dress. She was reputed to be "intense". She must have been one of the last survivals of the aesthetic movement which had flourished in the 1880's.

The curriculum of the kindergarten was rather heavily weighted on the literary and aesthetic side, although number-work was

taught with the assistance of counters and a ball-frame. There
was no kind of nature-study or outdoor "walks", nor was there
any opportunity for a small boy to develop his interest in machinery. For that I had to rely on my illustrated *Discoveries and Inventions of the Nineteenth Century*. However, some practical experience of contemporary scientific progress was afforded by an
excursion, early in 1891, on the recently opened City and South
London Railway. This was the first of the London electric underground lines, and it ran from King William Street, near London
Bridge, under the Thames, and eventually to Stockwell. The
locomotive and carriages fitted closely into the tunnels, which
were much narrower than those of our present-day "tubes"; and
for this reason the carriages, which had no windows, cannot have
been more than 8 feet across, and a tall man could hardly stand
upright in them. It was a great adventure to sample this new
method of transport. Another event which has impressed itself
on my memory was a visit to the Naval Exhibition of 1891.
Exhibitions of this type were held almost every year in London
during the last decade of the nineteenth century—usually at
Earls Court or Olympia. The Naval Exhibition included a
replica of a lighthouse, some 200 feet high, with a lantern lighted
at night by electricity. There was also a building, disguised as an
iceberg, which housed a number of pictures and panoramas illus-
trative of Arctic discovery. In addition to all this there were
innumerable models of ships of all kinds, and a stretch of water in
which miniature gunboats had mock engagements. At intervals
squads of blue-jackets gave displays of drill and dancing.

The large garden, the life of my grandfather's household, the
seaside holidays and the interests fostered by my new experiences
at school all made life at Thornton Heath very pleasant for an only
child—a boy aged 6 to 7. Sometimes I had a visitor all of my own.
His name was Alan Milne, and he afterwards became famous as
the creator of *Winnie the Pooh*, and many another entrancing and
whimsical fancy. His governess and mine were sisters, and that is
how the introduction was effected. But these happy days were
destined not to last. In 1890 my mother came home after wintering

at Ventnor, and she died a week later. In the last year or so of her life she had been nursed and cared for by a "lady companion", who after her death stayed on in order to look after me. In due course she became my stepmother, and she watched over my childhood and youth with unceasing care. Of my mother herself I have only a faint recollection—a dim picture of a young woman in a black dress, with a bunch of keys attached to a chain hanging from her girdle, and with her hair smoothed tightly back from her forehead and tied into a knot behind. But from her correspondence, which many years later came into my hands, she became more real to me; and I saw how close had been the link between her and my grandfather, and with what courage and faith she had endured the illness which led to her early death. But at the time her departure made little difference to me, for I had seen her only at rare intervals since we left London. The real break came a year and a half later. One morning, when I was playing some solitary jungle game among the bushes and trees in the front garden, I saw a policeman come up the drive to the front door. He brought the news that my grandfather had had a heart attack in a cab on his way from Victoria to the L.C.C. offices which were then situated in Spring Gardens, near the Embankment. He was taken to Charing Cross Hospital, but died before he arrived there. This event entailed a complete change in my life and a temporary depreciation of the family fortunes. The house at Thornton Heath was taken over by my grandfather's eldest son; and my father, together with me and my future stepmother as house-keeper and foster-mother, migrated to a suburb of north-west London. There we settled down in a small, semi-detached house—"pokey villa", as my father used to call it—one of a whole series, each the counterpart of the other, and with a strip of garden devoid even of any trees. A new chapter in my life had indeed begun.

CHAPTER 5

# Suburbia

I WAS destined to live in this suburb—though not all the time in "pokey" villa—for the rest of my childhood and youth, and even after I had gone up to Oxford I still spent a good part of the vacations there. Although building was going on rapidly it was still near enough to open country of sorts to make possible expeditions among fields and along footpaths. Life in Suburbia was an enormous contrast to the conditions at Thornton Heath; but a child soon becomes acclimatised, and there was always something interesting going on in the road.

Many commodities were retailed by itinerant tradesmen who shouted their wares. The cats'-meat man, for example, was a familiar figure in those days when the numerous varieties of pet-foods in tins were unknown. He used to trundle a barrow full of pieces of horsemeat skewered on small sticks. At the sound of his long drawn out cry of "Ca-a-ats' me-e-at" and perhaps the scent of his wares, all the cats of the neighbourhood came running out and he was usually followed by a train of them as he made his slow progress up the street. Then there was the coal-man whose cry sounded like "Oh Miss Cromer, Chronico!" but I never discovered what he really meant. Milk at "tuppence 'apenny a quart" was delivered by an insanitary process which has fortunately been replaced by the present system of milk in bottles. A metal churn containing several gallons was carried around, and when the milkman called at one's house the maid would take out a jug and the required amount would be ladled out by means of a

scoop holding half-a-pint. There was no guarantee against dust or
dirt contaminating the milk during this process. The muffin-man,
with his bell and tray on his head, was a feature of winter afternoons—I am glad that he is not yet quite obsolete. Some of the
old street-cries remained. How well I remember:*

Will ye buy my sweet blooming lavender ?    Fifteen    fine    branches a    penny..........

A less elaborate chant was that of the "Catch 'em all alive" man.
In those days house flies were far more in evidence than they are
today, and it was customary to hang up sheets of paper covered
with some sticky substance. This attracted the flies and held them
fast, so that they were condemned to a lingering death. The
vender of these sheets had one of them, plentifully stuck over
with flies, displayed round his hat, and he paraded the streets
singing

> Oh, those troublesome flies!
> Catch 'em all alive.

Then there were the professional musicians. The street-piano
visited us regularly once a week. It had a repertoire of all the
favourite popular tunes; chief among them was "Ta-ra-ra-boom-
deay", which was sung and played everywhere in the early
1890's. Sometimes we would be entertained by a "one-man-
band". Here the performer had a big drum strapped to his back,
and he beat it by means of drum-sticks strapped to his elbows.
On top of it were cymbals operated by strings connected with his
heels. In front he had a set of pan-pipes fixed to his chest, and his
hands were occupied with a concertina. Round the rim of his hat
were bells. He was a popular figure. Occasionally a highlander in
full costume would delight (?) us with selections on the bagpipes;
and he was usually accompanied by a young lady who performed

* Vaughan Williams introduces a variant of this street-cry into his opera
*Hugh the Drover.*

Scottish dances in the middle of the road. At other times we would be visited by a "German band"—four or five wind-instrument players who specialised on selections from opera. A pathetic contrast to all these, who brought a measure of cheerfulness into our suburb, was the down-and-out unemployed (or unemployable) who walked slowly up the middle of the road singing hymns. These were usually of the most lugubrious type. One of the most popular was that gruesome production of the poet Cowper which begins:

> There is a Fountain filled with blood
> Drawn from Emmanuel's veins;
> And sinners, plunged beneath the flood,
> Lose all their guilty stains.

It was when we went to live in Suburbia that I was introduced to the "popular song". Each year we had at least one of these and they were sung by errand boys and known to everybody. Unlike the vacuous cacophony which passes as popular music nowadays, these songs contained a recognisable and usually attractive tune and were constructed with some regard to form and harmony. I have already referred to "ta-ra-ra-boom-deay" which had been popularised by a music-hall actress called Lottie Collins. It was really just an accompaniment to a dance, but these songs very often had some contemporary reference. One, which seems to have survived and to which even now one sometimes sees a reference, concerned the new-fangled spectacle of the woman-bicyclist—

> Daisy, Daisy, give me your answer true
> I'm half crazy, all for the love of you.
> It won't be a stylish marriage,
> For I can't afford a carriage.
> But you'll look sweet, upon the seat
> Of a bicycle made for two.

When motors first appeared on the highways* a well-known music-hall artist, named Harry Tate, popularised a song which

* See below, pp. 77–78.

described how the car driver was anxious to propose to his lady passenger; but—

> A dozen times of love he'd try to speak
> And then the radiator it would leak,
>     so . . .
> He had to get under,
> Get out and get under.

The next stage was the aeroplane which was celebrated thus:

> O Dorothy, Dorothy D.
> O Dorothy, where can she be?
> She's suddenly flown
> To regions unknown
> Along with a man on a flying machine.

Sometimes the song dealt with some popular or familiar figure, e.g. the policeman or the railway porter. Although the former was guyed in the *Pirates of Penzance* (which was first produced in 1880) he was never really a figure of fun. It was no uncommon sight to see a line of policemen, in single file and headed by their sergeant, marching along the pavement on their way to their respective beats. This accounts for the way they make their entry on to the stage in the play. So the policeman was a friend to be consulted when one had a problem—

> If you want to know the time ask a p'liceman—
> Proper Greenwich time—ask a p'liceman.
> Every member of the force
> Has a watch and chain of course,
> If you want to know the time, ask a p'liceman.

Another year we celebrated the porter who was called in to advise the young lady who ventured on a train journey un-chaperoned—

> O Mr. Porter, what shall I do?
> I wanted to go to Birmingham and they've taken me on to Crewe
> Send me back to London as quickly as you can
> O Mr. Porter, what a silly girl I am!

Not only were popular songs much in evidence in those late Victorian days, but advertisement slogans also seemed to "catch on" easily. With my father's co-operation and as a kind of joke I used to look out for these and made a collection of them. Everyone knew of Dr. Williams' Pink Pills for Pale People and had read—sometimes with amusement and sometimes with incredulity—the published excerpts from the letters of grateful patients who had benefited from them. Others owed their miraculous cure to Beecham's Pills which were "worth a guinea a box". I wonder if they still are. Wright's Coal Tar soap was associated with a picture of a baby in a hip-bath who is reaching for a cake of this compound and "won't be happy till he gets it". Another slogan that occurs to me is:

> They come as a boon and a blessing to men—
> The Pickwick, the Owl and the Waverley pen.

For those were the days of steel nibs in pen-holders. The fountain or reservoir pen was not in general use and the biro of course had not been invented. Even during my Oxford days (1903–10) some colleges still provided quill pens for the benefit of undergraduates who wanted to take notes during lectures. At school we used to take a malicious delight in putting carbide (used in bicycle acetylene lamps) into the inkwells. This produced a thick jelly which was quite useless for writing purposes.

I have mentioned some of the agencies which enlivened street-life in our suburb, but sometimes an interest of quite a different kind would be introduced. Every now and then a funeral would come up our road. It was a solemn procession proceeding at a walking pace. First came the hearse drawn by two jet-black horses who often wore black plumes on their heads. On each side walked two of the undertaker's staff, called "mutes", who were accoutred in frock coats and top-hats. Behind the coffin came the coaches of the mourners, and these were also drawn by black horses. The wearing of mourning was strictly *de rigeur* in our middle class society. The length to which it was carried depended on the nearness of one's relationship to the departed, and also on how long had elapsed since his decease. Widows in particular were attired in the deepest black, with crêpe trimmings, and the whole get up was known as "weeds". Eventually one was allowed to relax somewhat and to wear "semi-mourning". For a man it was usually sufficient to appear in subfusc clothes and a black tie; and one often had a black hat-band, the depth of which (according to *Punch*) was determined according to whether one was mentioned in the will or not. In any case one would have an arm-band of crêpe, about 3 or 4 inches deep, on one's left sleeve until the period of mourning was at an end.

In the 1880's and 1890's the custom of cremating the bodies of the dead was gradually coming into use though it was by no means common. The great Necropolis at Woking dates from 1885, and in it is the oldest of our crematoria. But in the early years of the twentieth century others were opened in many of our cities and large towns, and the provision of them has greatly increased ever since. Nowadays if one looks down the obituary columns of *The Times* one can see that the number of cremations often equals, if it does not exceed, that of interments. So here is yet another change in middle-class customs that has been effected during my lifetime. Yet cremation had to encounter a good deal of opposition and prejudice, especially in the early stages. The Bishop of Lincoln, for example, preached in Westminster Abbey a violent sermon condemning the practice because it would "undermine the faith of mankind in the doctrine of the resurrection of the body". One wonders how things would be arranged in the case of the holy martyrs who were burned at the stake.

All these experiences of life in the suburbs were quite new to me. Another fresh interest was provided by the school to which I was now sent. It was carried on in a fair-sized private house and was described on the brass-plate at the front gate as a "School for the Sons of Gentlemen". There were two school-rooms. In one corner of the larger of these sat the headmistress—an imposing dame of ample proportions, wearing a lace cap and elaborately upholstered in the costume affected by elderly ladies of the period. She was the sister of a well-known publisher of evangelical

leanings and the author of several improving books. Remainders
bearing the imprint of his firm figured largely among the prizes
which were lavishly distributed at the end of the school year.
There were about thirty pupils, all boys, with a small proportion
of boarders. The principal was assisted by two young women—
though I doubt whether any of the three would have qualified
for "Q.T." status. One of them was a pleasant person whom we
all liked, but the other (like Queen Victoria) had a permanent expression of being not amused. In addition to the two assistant-
mistresses a certain Dr. Spear appeared periodically to teach
Latin. I remember once seeing a yellow note-book of his, on the
cover of which was written "Oliver Spear, LL.D. (Lond.)"; and
asking my father the meaning of the mysterious suffix. I have
sometimes wondered how a legal doctor came to be a visiting
teacher of the rudiments of Latin in a suburban private school for
small boys.

As I have said, there were a few boarders at this school and for
a short time I joined them. We all slept in a large bedroom and
were under the eye of the senior assistant mistress whose bedroom
was next door. I think we were quite well looked after, but the
meals included some rather curious items. Bread and syrup was
one of the stand-bys at breakfast and tea. At mid-day dinner suet
pudding in various disguises was provided to stay the pangs of
hunger; but I have a particularly vivid recollection of what were
called "vegetables". These consisted of leguminous, brassic or
tuberous oddments of all sorts (fragments left over from previous
meals?) which had been mashed up into a greenish-grey mass of
not very appetising appearance. If one were asked "Will you have
some vegetables?" one acquiesced without enthusiasm and was
then served with a dollop of the mixture in which one might
actually come across unmashed lumps of carrot or turnip or
cabbage-stalk which betrayed the heterogeneous nature of the
compound.

The only playground was an asphalted yard and no organised
games or any form of physical education figured in the curriculum. Those of us, however, who took dancing as an "extra"

profited by the visits of a certain Miss Dives who put us through our paces on Wednesday afternoon—a holiday for the other pupils. The class consisted entirely of boys and was held in the larger of the two school-rooms, with the chairs and tables pushed back. We learnt the polka and the quadrille, the waltz and the lancers. The dancing class afforded ample opportunity for a display of animal spirits, of which we took full advantage and which Miss Dives was not always able to control. For example, the "ladies' chain" in the lancers gave one a chance to pull the next fellow over when one took his hand, and the resultant mêlée more often resembled a game of rugby than an orthodox dancing lesson. I acquired some kudos on one occasion by unbuttoning the strap of my dancing-shoe, so that with a slight kick it flew off into the air and smashed a gas-globe. In such ways as these we managed to extract some enjoyment from our dancing lessons, even though they were held on half-holidays. But once a term, as a civilising and refining influence, a few little girls of our own age were brought in to be our partners. It was an occasion for dismay and gloom. We were struck dumb and with difficulty performed the prescribed rituals. Great was our relief when the time came for us to lead our partners up to Miss Dives—we bowing and they curtseying to the strains of Boccherini's *Minuet in A*; for this was invariably the last exercise of the afternoon. Yet amongst us there was one renegade—a fellow called Cooper—who actually seemed to enjoy these occasions. He was even seen talking to girls, apparently completely at his ease. As might be expected, he wore a tweed suit and a stiff white collar. But he heard all about it next morning when he became a figure of scorn and a common mocking-stock.

I could read easily by the time I reached this school; and it was here that I was introduced to the gems of English literature contained in a collection of short passages of informative or didactic prose. These were interspersed with poems of the "Wreck of the *Hesperus*" or "Inchcape Rock" type. To each excerpt a list of spellings was appended. The art of writing was fostered by regular practice with copy-books in which one reproduced, as well as one could, copper-plate maxims such as "Honesty is the best policy" or "Flee evil companions". Arithmetic (known as "sums") was worked on slates with a squeaky pencil and an un-hygienic fragment of sponge, attached to the slate by a string and used for rubbing out (it was necessary to suck it first). We used Cornwell's *Geography* and Mrs. Markham's *History of England*, with its conversations at the end of each chapter. The information given in both alike was essentially factual; it had to be learnt and was then "heard". But part of the instruction was given by means of catechisms, where both question and answer had to be committed to memory. We had such compendiums for Scripture and General Knowledge, and Mangnall's *Questions* still survived. One learnt a page at a time. On one occasion the page in the Scripture book ended thus: "Q. What did they then do? A. They gave Him vinegar to drink. Q. What did He then say? A. It is finished". When my father, who was hearing me my homework, asked "What was finished?" I naturally replied "The vinegar". The first couplet on the next page ran: "Q. What was finished? A. Man's redemption"—which in any case would have been quite incomprehensible.

As well as learning these catechisms we were required to get by heart spelling lists, arithmetical tables, the Kings of England and their dates, counties and county towns with their rivers, the books of the Bible, lists of the Apostles and the Jewish tribes—in fact any information which could be reduced to tabular form. We also learnt the Ten Commandments, selected Psalms, the Apostles' Creed, the Beatitudes, Collects. So far as I can remember no ex-planations were ever given; but I have never ceased to be grateful that, at an age when memorisation is easy, I acquired a store of such things. However little they may have meant to me at the time, I came to value them later and they have remained a valuable possession all my life. In particular I am glad to have been made to learn collects from the Prayer Book. They surely en-shrine the spirit of devotion.

When I reached the age of 9 I began to learn Latin and to profit from the visits of Dr. Spear. To my tale of rote-work were added declensions, conjugations, vocabularies and rules. Yet I am sure that I never resented my question and answer catechisms or my tabulated lists or principal parts. After all, in those days it was understood that one went to school to *learn* things, and not to be entertained. Saying off a memorised screed was like a porter calling out the list of stations as the train came in. To have acquired if only a table of words or a formula gave one a certain sense of power. A cousin of mine, of about my own age, learnt off the names of the Dukes of Edom, as given in Genesis, chapter 36, and also $\pi$ to I don't know how many places—just for the fun of the thing. So I soon got hold of *mensa* and *amo*, and all the other forms to which I was introduced in Dr. Smith's *Principia Latina*; and before long I was translating such sentences as "The queen gives an eagle to the husbandman"—though I had no idea what a husbandman was, and it never occurred to me to ask. Between the learned doctor's visits our Latin studies (and we eventually reached simplified Caesar) were overseen by the sour-faced assistant mistress whose knowledge of the language was commensurate with our own. Once she overheard one of us say to his neighbour "*She* told us (so and so)"; whereat she asked rather acidly "Who is *she*?" To which the whole class, by a kind of reflex action and without the least malice, replied "The cat's mother".

No form of drawing or art or craft-work was taught in this school; but every boy, whether he had any aptitude or not, learnt to play the piano. In those days, when one went to a children's party, one was expected to contribute to the evening's entertainment; so that "accomplishments" were of some social importance. We started with an Instruction Book. After some preliminary practice with scales and arpeggios we passed on to airs such as *The Bluebells of Scotland* or *Rousseau's Dream*, with a simple harmonisation, or to fragments from Italian operas boiled down for the use of beginners and provided with a "tum-tum-tum" or Alberti bass accompaniment. But, once free from the Instruction Book, the neophyte was promoted to "pieces". These included such gems as Sydney Smith's *Waves of the Ocean* and Gustav Lange's *Blumenlied*. All the same, one had acquired the main rudiments of music and had gained some experience of a keyboard instrument. With me it meant an introduction to what became a life long devotion.

Although no physical education was provided by the school this did not mean that we were deprived of exercise. In spite of the fact that we were assumed to be "sons of gentlemen" we were not above playing in the street; and in any case the open country was not far away. It was in the fields beyond the end of our road that we played a game which consisted in pretending to be pre-historic animals, called for some reason or other, "gitrons". All one did was to range about and then suddenly fall upon someone else crying "I'll clunge you fosta mungles" which was supposed to mean "I'll tear you into pieces". Then we just wrestled until one or the other (or both) of us fell over; and then one got up and went through the same performance all over again. It sounds rather pointless, but somehow small boys can get a good deal of enjoyment out of seemingly futile activities of this kind.

Ordinary street-games, if I mistake not, were much more in evidence than they are today, and they followed a seasonal rhythm. In winter hoops were popular. Girls had wooden ones, driven by a stick. They tended easily to get out of control and ran the risk of suddenly going off at a tangent into the road and perhaps becoming involved with the legs of a passing horse. But boys used iron hoops, controlled by a hook called a "skimmer", which could be used not only as a propellant but also as a brake. A good run with a hoop in frosty weather was admirable exercise and one of my favourite occupations. Later on came the turn of the peg-top (for some reason or other we never used whip-tops). This was operated by a cord tightly wound round, and it re-quired some knack to throw the contraption so that the top spun steadily upright on its peg. If it kept in this position it was called a "sleeper". One could even play a game the object of which was to split one's opponent's top by striking it with the peg of one's own; but the best tops were made of hard box-wood which could resist any attack. Autumn was the season of "conkers"—

but that is a game which has survived. Hop-scotch (which also seems still to be practised) was patronised in some quarters, but not by us because it involved chalking on the pavement, and that was considered to be "vulgar". Marbles also, for some unknown reason, was regarded as *infra dig*. We did, however, play counting-out games which involved eliminating the "he" who, under given conditions—as, for example, in "touch"—had to catch the other participants. The counting-out was done by means of traditional rhymes two of which remain in my memory:

> Eena, meena, mina, muss
> Cattla, weela, wila, wuss,
> Spit, spot, must be done
> Twiddlum, twaddlum, twenty-one.
> O – U – T spells out
> With a dirty dish-clout.
> Out goes *he*.

The other runs as follows:

> 1, 2, 3, 4, 5, 6, 7
> All good children go to heaven.
> Penny on the water,
> Twopence on the sea,
> Threepence on the railway
> Out goes *he*.

I suppose that the rhymes and the games with which they are associated still survive in the playgrounds of primary schools. It would be a pity if these counting-out jingles, some of which must be of considerable antiquity and which are found in many other countries besides our own, should fall to any extent into abeyance. If one suddenly wanted to contract out of the conditions under which the game was being played, one shouted "fainitz". The derivation and distribution of this extraordinary word have been investigated by Iona and Peter Opie in their *The Lore and Language of School Children*.* It seems to be confined to London and southern England and to be a survival from medieval English.

* See pp. 140–53, and especially p. 151.

It was at about the age of 11 that I learnt to ride a bicycle. A year before that I had been given a tricycle—a horrible affair with solid tyres, and a big wheel on one side and two small ones on the other. The rider held on to two handles, one on each side, and steered the machine by twisting them. Solid-tyre cycles were still common; I remember once being knocked down at Thornton Heath by a "penny-farthing" bicycle—a machine with a front wheel some 5 feet in diameter and the rider perched high in the air on top of it. But the "safety" bicycle was already in use, and the pneumatic tyre was rapidly taking the place of the old solid or cushion tyre. So my new bicycle was one of the latest pattern; and after a few preliminary pushes by my father up and down our road I soon learnt to ride alone, and—like the boy in H. C. Beeching's poem—I was "free" in another element.

Indoors I continued to give a good deal of my spare time to reading. I was particularly fond of fairy-tales and got together a number of these—Hans Andersen, Grimm, D'Aulnoy and the various coloured collections edited by Andrew Lang. But another interest was an imaginary country called Sluckeslond, of which I was the King. I still possess several quarto exercise books (dated 1893 and costing one-halfpenny each) filled with details connected with this phantasy. To begin with there is an elementary grammar of the Sluckeslondish language, together with "volcabuaries", which bear a family likeness to the Latin which I was already learning. A feature of the grammar is a list of "conarcles", defined as "words not nouns, pronouns, adjectives or verbs". This is followed by a list of weights and measures almost as complicated as those which I was getting by heart at school. Then comes a map of the country, the capital of which was called Bingidong. There is also a history from the year 1135 when Sluckeslond was conquered from the "Pnomes and Mnomes". There follows a list of Kings, with dates, and against each name is a "character"—somewhat after the fashion of the historical books of the Old Testament. Next is a table of events from which it appears that in this country railways were invented in 1270, torpedos in 1312, ink in 1370, prayer-books in 1420, saucepans in 1474, wallpaper in 1490 and "queneen" in 1572. The kings seem to have emulated the exploits of some of their counterparts in real life. We read, for example, of a ruler who in 1301 was responsible for the "burning of 3000 souls", and in 1319 for "cutting eyes out of 190 souls". Another king killed ten bishops "for saying that he was a hog". After this précis of history come illustrations of Sluckeslondish soldiers, the terminus of the Bingidong and South Western Railway, the palace at Wegedong, and the organ in Bingidong Cathedral. On the front of this latter is the appropriate inscription TE DEUM LAUDAMUS, which I must have copied out of the Prayer Book. There is a note to say that the organist's name is Fremac Zanfer Almons—which is somehow reminiscent of *Gulliver's Travels*. It all seemed very real at the time; but when one looks back upon it, or turns over the pages of the exercise books in which these details are recorded, the whole business suggests a parody of the education which I was receiving at the "School for the Sons of Gentlemen".

CHAPTER 6

# Holidays

MY STEPMOTHER's father had made some money as a contractor for the building of the Portsmouth "Lines" and part of the London underground railway. When he retired on the proceeds he bought a farm at Bishop's Waltham, near Winchester. I am not sure that he knew a great deal about agriculture, and I suspect that as a gentleman-farmer he lost much of the fortune which he had acquired. But it was a periodic delight to me to visit his farm, and it brought a wealth of new experiences to which, as a town-dweller, I had hitherto been a stranger. Along one border of the farm ran a stream where a kingfisher lived. From there it sloped up to a ridge along the top of which ran a copse. Here, if one were lucky, one might see a wild cat—the descendant of a feline colony which had established itself in one of the sheds where the agricultural machines were kept. Occasionally one of the brood would take to the wild and revert to its ancestral habits.

The farmhouse itself was a modern and commodious building. It had two kitchens, in one of which was a brick oven. When this was used it was first of all filled with faggots, and when these had burnt themselves out the embers were withdrawn. Then the loaves and cakes and pies were put in by means of a kind of wooden shovel. The result was very successful, except that some-times one would find a piece of wood-ash stuck on one's slice of bread or cake. At the farm I used to sleep on a feather mattress in an old four-poster bed with a tester over my head. On the reredos —or whatever the headboard at the back is called—there were

two watch-pockets; and in one of these I would usually find a
bun or a piece of cake, put there by my kind hostess (my stepmother's mother) in case I should wake up early and feel hungry.
The main activity of the farm was dairying. The raw milk was
brought in pails from the cow-house and poured into a refrigera-
tor, through which a stream of cold water flowed. The milk
itself, by some process which was a perpetual marvel to me,
trickled down over a vertical, corrugated surface, without falling
off onto the floor; and it was then transferred to large metal
churns. A journey to the station in the milk-cart, drawn by a
fast-trotting pony called Daphne, and with three or four churns
aboard, was one of the chief attractions of a holiday on the farm.

On Sunday morning everyone who could be spared from the
work of the farm went to church; and when the weather was fine
the journey was made on foot, although the distance both ways
must have been well over 4 miles. The service seemed an inter-
minable business. There was no choir, but the psalms and canticles
were recited antiphonally by the parson and the congregation.
We did, however, sing hymns to the accompaniment of an organ
which stood in one of the aisles, half-way down the church and in
full view of the congregation. When the office was ended the
parson retired to the vestry at the west-end of the church, and
shortly afterwards reappeared wearing a black academic gown
instead of his surplice. I have never been able to fathom the
significance of this particular piece of ritualism. The country
rector in those days was often himself as much a farmer as a
parson. My stepmother's father, who was a churchwarden, used
to relate how on one occasion he and the rector had bargained on
and off all through the week about the sale of a pig. On the
following Sunday morning, as the parson walked up the church
having assumed his black gown, he paused at the pew, at the
corner of which his churchwarden was sitting, and muttered in an
undertone "I'll give you five pounds for the pig". Then he continued his way to the pulpit. The tedium of the sermon was
beguiled by the sucking of "curiously strong" peppermints, of
which the churchwarden's wife kept a store with the prayer-

books in a small box at the end of the pew. On Sunday evenings no one went to church; but the whole household gathered in the dining-room, where my stepmother's father read the collect for the day and the lessons for evensong. We also sang familiar hymns—always the same ones—"Sun of my soul", "Abide with me", "Glory to Thee, my God, this night". The age of faith still survived in this rural setting.

My experiences of country life were supplemented by periodic visits to the Leith Hill neighbourhood in Surrey. My paternal grandfather (the one who lived at Canonbury) had a small country cottage near Holmbury St. Mary, and during the middle part of the year some members of the family were usually taking their holidays there. If there was insufficient accommodation some of us would be boarded out in neighbouring cottages or at the Holly-bush inn at Holmbury. The whole area is surely one of the most delectable parts of England, and even today, in spite of the advent of the motor-car and the easy accessibility of the Surrey Hills to London, it retains much of its charm. In my boyhood the district had hardly at all been "developed" as a holiday resort or as a residential area for the well-to-do. It had lost little of its rural—not to say rustic—character. One could even occasionally see a local inhabitant wearing a smock frock. The centuries-old social set-up was also still in evidence. The local magnate was the "squire"—in this case Squire Evelyn (as he was always called), who lived at Wotton House, just off the Guildford–Dorking main road and not far from Abinger. He was a descendant of the diarist, John Evelyn, who had lived there in the times of the Stuart Kings. The Squire was a figure of great importance in the rural community. When he came along the road in his dog-cart, the tenants would stand respectfully at the side, doffing their hats as he passed. But Evelyn was at any rate a benevolent despot and kept his dependants' cottages in good order. There were land-owners who allowed their tenants to live under insanitary conditions in cottages with leaky roofs and ill-fitting windows; but Evelyn was not one of those. All the same, the life of the agri-cultural labourer in those days was a hard one. He had none of the assistance which is now afforded by tractors, combine harvesters and other mechanical aids. The average cash wages of an agricultural labourer in Surrey in the period 1892–3 was 15/– a week, but in some counties (e.g. Berkshire and Dorset) they were as low as 10/–;* but living accommodation, a piece of vegetable garden, a supply of faggots, and perhaps an allowance of beer, were often provided in addition. But, generally speaking, the period of my boyhood was one of agricultural depression, although the industry was slowly reviving. However, life for many farm-workers—especially those who lived at some distance from the nearest village—must have tended to be self-centred and stagnant. Easy means of communication, such as can be provided today by the motor-car, were not available, and children (instead of being collected in omnibuses) often had to walk long distances to and from school, and in all sorts of weather. The fairs which travelled round the countryside afforded some periodic amusement, and their successors remain to this day. There was usually a roundabout, sometimes operated by a man turning a wheel, but more often by a steam-engine which also kept in motion an "organ". This emitted raucous music all the time that the roundabout was revolving. There were many side-shows—the bearded lady, the African giant, and so on—and also stalls from which Johnny "promised to buy me a bunch of blue ribbon". The social conditions of the agricultural labourer and his family have been vastly improved during more recent times by the foundation of village community centres and by such associations as the Women's Institutes which date from 1915.

So much for the summer holidays. My chief winter treat was to go to the pantomime. My grandfather's younger brother, who was a bachelor, had spent most of his life in the Indian Civil Service, and he had a fund of anecdotes relating to the Far East which made him a great favourite with his young relatives and friends. Every year he used to invite them to the Christmas pantomime at Drury Lane Theatre, which was then under the

* See the tables in Onwin and Felton, *A Century of Wages and Earnings in Agriculture.*

management of Sir August Harris. *Punch* used to call him "Druriolanus". We were usually accommodated in a box. The girls sat in front, while the boys filled up the back of the box, from which it was not always easy to get a clear view of the stage. The chief attraction from our point of view was the comedians— Herbert Campbell and Dan Leno. The former was tall and big, and used to take the "Widow Twankie" roles; while the latter was short and slight—rather like Charlie Chaplin. On one occasion Herbert Campbell, as the mother, had to give Dan Leno, as her son, a bath. Drying was achieved by putting the latter through the mangle, as if he had been a sheet or blanket. Then Herbert Campbell took a towel and twisted it up into a long, thin roll which somehow or other kept stiff. This he inserted into one of Dan Leno's ears, and twisted it round and round until at last it came out at the other ear! I have often wondered since how these illusions were produced.

Winter in Suburbia was also the time for Christmas parties. Anything more than just "going out to tea" involved a third-person invitation. One arrived in one's best clothes (I had by this time been promoted to an Eton suit, vulgarly known as a "bum-freezer"), wearing white cotton gloves and carrying one's "music". In those days we provided our own entertainment (unless one of the fathers gave a magic-lantern show), and everyone was expected to make his or her contribution. This, as I have already said, explains the social importance of the piano lessons which I was receiving at my private school. The performances may not have reached a high level, but at any rate they were an activity. Our instrumental and vocal efforts were interspersed with round games such as "Musical Chairs", "Hunt the Slipper", or "General Post". Often there was dancing which always ended with "Sir Roger de Coverley". It seems a great pity that this delightful and traditional English dance should now have gone out of fashion.

On one occasion I was invited to the annual fancy-dress children's ball, given at the Mansion House by the Lord Mayor of London. The father of one of my aunts by marriage (the one for whom I had acted as page) was the Lord Mayor's Sword Bearer; and it was doubtless from this source that the invitation came. I was disguised as Robin Hood; but I do not remember having taken much part in the dancing. Instead I spent a good deal of time playing up and down a staircase with two other boys. All the same there was a conjurer and a magnificent supper, and finally a march-past of all the young guests in front of the Lord Mayor who was wearing his full regalia. On another occasion I was privileged to see the Lord Mayor's show from a seat on the front of the Mansion House. The procession included a life-boat and several tableaux representing City Companies—including the Goldsmiths. There were also a number of men dressed as court-cards, like the illustrations in *Alice in Wonderland*. At the end came the gilt coach containing the Lord Mayor himself, together with his Sword Bearer and his Mace Bearer. It was the former of these two officials who interested me most—my aunt's father in full robes and wearing a tall, furry, biretta-shaped hat; and holding the huge, ornamented sword which typified the Lord Mayor's power of administering justice within the City.

## CHAPTER 7

# Henderson's

THE kindergarten and the dame's school which have been described in the last two chapters were, of course, fee-paying establishments and, as such, were associated with the middle-class stratum of society in which I had been brought up. But for the children of the "lower classes" there was the board school or the voluntary school in which education was, or could be, free. Thus there were two parallel educational streams, and it was difficult—in many cases impossible—to get from the second stream into the first. Once you started on the state-aided, mainly free, elementary course you stayed in it unless you had exceptional luck or grit. Similarly, if you embarked upon the independent, fee-paying secondary course you went through with it. There was normally little question of "aptitude", so long as the fees were paid. The situation fostered, and was fostered by, contemporary social attitudes. "Board school" was a term of contempt in my "middle-class" suburban milieu; and one said "board-school boy" much as Swift's houyhnhnms used the term "yahoo". The products of these establishments were looked down upon as being shabby and dirty urchins, who shouted in the street and could not speak the Queen's English; whereas we were "sons of gentlemen" and knew how to behave (or thought we did). It would have been considered an unspeakable disgrace if one of us had had to be transferred to an "elementary" school. This attitude towards the "board school" and its successors persisted in certain quarters long after 1902, when this type of institution officially ceased to exist. I am not sure that this form of snobbery has even yet completely disappeared, for the term "State school" still tends to convey a note of disapproval; but there has none the less been a notable advance in this respect during the last half-century. In any case our feelings were heartily reciprocated by the other side, and there was an almost perpetual feud between the two parties. I will remember being hit on the head by a doughty urchin of about my own age who exclaimed "You're a bleeding torf, ain't yer?" And so I doubtless was.

It was in this capacity, then, that at about the age of 11 I was transferred from the "School for the Sons of Gentlemen" to what frankly described itself as a "Preparatory School". It was a very select establishment and was usually known as "Henderson's", after the name of its headmaster who was an Edinburgh graduate. In the suburb where we lived there was a fairly large colony of well-to-do business men who had emigrated from Scotland and were making the most of their opportunities in London. They were staunch supporters of a local Presbyterian church, the minister of which rose to be one of the shining lights of his denomination. It was to this school that they sent their boys, and thus there was always a certain Scottish flavour about it which gave it a distinctive character. The school consisted entirely of day-boys, and was carried on in a large and convenient house, with a small playing-field attached. The headmaster was an enthusiast for good literature and was able to make us share his enthusiasm. It was through him that I was introduced to *The Tempest*, *Twelfth Night*, *Henry V*, and *A Midsummer Night's Dream*—though it was some years later that I paid my first visit to the theatre and saw Frank Benson and his company in *Antony and Cleopatra*. This was rather a concession because it was something of a tradition in the puritanical section of the Victorian middle class to look with severe disapproval on the theatre. But the best part of the week at Henderson's was on Friday afternoon when the Head used to read to us the novels of Stevenson and Dumas. The only punishment in vogue in the school was to be debarred from "reading"; and that in itself was sufficient to ensure that breaches of the school rules were rarely committed.

In spite of this emphasis on English we were well grounded in arithmetic, algebra and geometry (which we learnt from Euclid's *Elements*). History and geography continued to be taught by the memorisation of sheer facts. Latin bulked largely in the time-table; and as I had already started this subject at the dame's school I continued to make some progress with it. In a year or two I also began Greek, and was soon learning a new series of declensions and paradigms from W. Gunion Rutherford's grammar, or translating sentences from Ritchie's *First Steps in Greek*. With all this I started yet another language—French. This was taught by a lady who visited the school periodically (until she eventually married the headmaster). Her technique purported to be that devised by a certain Monsieur Gouin. It was apparently a forerunner of the "Direct Method", but I made little progress by means of it. Perhaps I was too much accustomed to the formal techniques by which the Classics were taught. The headmaster was assisted by a series of young men who usually stayed for a year or less and then departed. They were for the most part candidates for Holy Orders, who were filling in the time until they were old enough to be made deacon; or else they were mere youths who had recently left school and were about to proceed to the University. Some of them were quite effective and some completely incompetent. One of the best—and I remember him with gratitude—in due course became a prison chaplain. I hope that his experience as an usher in a preparatory school for small boys was of some assistance to him in such a capacity.

Not infrequently I stayed to lunch at Henderson's and the meal provided was on the whole more interesting than that which had been served at my previous school. At any rate, we were spared the heterogeneous mess known as "vegetables". However, even at meals food for the mind was not neglected. During lunch we used to play "spelling game". There would be some fifteen or twenty people round the table—members of staff and a number of pupils. As the meal progressed each in turn suggested a letter of the alphabet. The object was to build up a complete word, but to spin out the process as long as possible. If by misadventure or inevitably one gave a letter which completed a word, one lost a "life". If one suspected that a suggested letter was given merely to prolong the issue and no possible word could result, one said "I challenge you". If the person challenged could substantiate his contribution by declaring the word at which he was aiming he got an extra point and the challenger lost a "life"; but if he was unable to do this the result went the opposite way. It all sounds complicated, but in fact it worked quite well and I do not think any of us disliked the exercise or felt that an attempt was being made to "improve" us.

We worked hard at this school. There was a good deal to learn and we were made to learn it. There was no teaching of science, but my aesthetic education was not neglected. I took "music" and "art", although both of these subjects were "extras", and not part of the regular curriculum. I had had the great advantage of coming from a musical family. My father was a keen amateur organist, and for many years he voluntarily gave up his Sunday afternoons in order to play for the chapel service of a large workhouse infirmary. He was also a member of the Handel Festival Choir, and we used to go regularly not only to the triennial festivals at the Crystal Palace, but also to the intermediate performances. Thus I early became familiar with the chief Handelian oratorios and I had a chance to hear such soloists as Charles Santley, Edward Lloyd, Adelina Patti, Mme Albani and Clara Butt. My mother as a young woman had had piano lessons at the Royal Academy; and one of my abiding recollections of her is lying in bed in the evening and hearing her play Schumann in the drawing-room downstairs. Several of my father's family were also musical—one sister was an L.R.A.M., one brother played the 'cello and another the flute, and one was an actor in the D'Oyly Carte Company and included Jack Point in his repertoire. So there was always plenty of music on that side of the family. On my mother's side, too, the tradition was pretty strong. One of my cousins—her brother's son—founded a choir and an orchestra which he still conducts and which not infrequently gives performances at the Albert Hall and the Royal Festival Hall. So musically I had a flying start and was set an example to try to live up to; and I have always been thankful for that. As soon, therefore, as I entered the preparatory school, having already made a start with "music" (which in this context always meant having piano lessons), I became a pupil of a lady who visited the school once a week. She was an admirable teacher. She jettisoned with scorn the works of Sydney Smith and Gustav Lange; and promptly put me on to a course of Bach's Two-part Inventions and Suites, the simpler sonatas of Mozart and Beethoven, suitable excerpts from Corelli or Haydn or Scarlatti, varied by more modern works by composers such as Mendelssohn, Stephen Heller, Reinecke, Grieg—a choice but varied musical repertoire.

There was also an artistic tradition on my father's side. My great-uncle George was a water-colourist of some note and the author of a number of books dealing mainly with landscape paintings. My grandfather's brother Frederick also won some distinction as a black-and-white artist and even qualified for inclusion in the *Dictionary of National Biography*.\* He was a frequent contributor to *Punch* and the *Illustrated London News* and was also an illustrator of Dickens' works. I am told that when he was doing illustrations for an edition of *Pilgrim's Progress* he had to depict the jury at Vanity Fair. The names of most of them made it fairly easy to delineate their characters; but he said that the real crux came in the case of Mr. Facing Both Ways. One of my uncles was a ceramic artist in the employ of the Josiah Wedgwood firm. He also wrote several art books dealing with pottery and had charge of the Wedgwood Museum at Etruria. I suppose that all this ought to have stimulated me to take an interest in pictorial art; but my aesthetic leanings always lay strongly in the direction of music. In any case the teaching of art at my preparatory school left a good deal to be desired. No encouragement was given to imaginative work. Instead we were set to copy plaster casts of conventional flowers, shading in our drawings with messy crayon

---

\* See *D.N.B.*, Supplement 1, p. 128.

or charcoal; or else we did mathematical representations of spirals, complete with vanishing lines and other paraphernalia. Of the two I preferred the latter. That finished my art education, for after leaving the preparatory school I never had any further occasion or encouragement to express myself by means of pencil or brush.

It was at my preparatory school that I first learned to play organised games. They were, I am thankful to say, not regarded as a fetish to the extent which even yet is not uncommon in schools of this type. All the same, games were *taught* and taken almost as seriously as lessons in the class-room. There was a continual shouting of instructions and praise or blame (in my case, usually blame) as the game proceeded. If the first purpose of a game is that it affords an opportunity for enjoyment, then it was not fulfilled so far as I was concerned. Football gave one scope to run about in a rough and tumble, with less chance of interference from the master on the touch-line; but lessons in cricket engendered in me a rooted dislike of the game which I never overcame. This is not to say that I do not enjoy watching a cricket-match provided that the weather is warm and sunny, and especially if I am supplied with a deck-chair and (at the appropriate time) a cup of tea.

I found far more pleasure in roaming about the neighbouring countryside, and particularly in cycling. This latter form of exercise, however, was carried on under disadvantages which do not exist today. Even the main roads in my youth were covered with mud in wet weather and were thick with dust in dry. The surface was continually being worn away under the hoofs of horses, and the iron-rimmed wheels of vehicles. Even after the advent of pneumatic tyres a long cycle ride would produce considerable tenderness in the hinder parts; and the risk of punctures also tended to complicate a journey. If one travelled at a rate of over 15 miles an hour one ran the risk of being summoned for "scorching". But the chief drawback was the dirt. If it was wet one got splashed with mud; but even worse in dry weather were the clouds of dust which rose up at the least provocation,

permeating one's clothing and filling one's lungs. In towns some
attempt to deal with the dust problem was made by the use of
water-carts. These consisted of tanks mounted on four wheels
and drawn by a horse. At the back there was a perforated sprinkler
extending the whole width of the cart, and when the driver
pressed down a lever the machine came into operation and the
surface of the road was bedewed with moisture as the water-cart
moved along. It was not unknown for street urchins to seek a
gratuitous ride by sitting on the sprinkler; but as soon as the
water was turned on they received a sort of hip bath. Water-carts
certainly had the effect of laying the dust and that was a great
advantage, but it also tended to turn the dust into mud and so
to produce a slippery surface which might be dangerous for
horses. In any case they were not used on country roads where
they were really most needed. However, as we had never known
the advantages of a tar-surfaced motor-road we were not de-
terred by these experiences. It became my ambition to see how
long a journey I could perform in a day. On one occasion, when
I was aged about 13, I rode from the farm at Bishop's Waltham
to a house at Finchley where my cousins were then living. The
distance must be about 75 miles. When I went into a shop at
Hook for something to eat the proprietor and his wife looked at
me curiously and catechised me as to whence I had come and
whither I was going. I am sure that they thought I had run away
from school; and when the time came for me to pay the bill they
refused to take anything from me.

My chief indoor activities at this time were reading and
playing the piano. We had a large collection of music at home
and I used to try my hand at it more or less indiscriminately. No
doubt this improved my capacity to play at sight, but it must
have been rather trying for the other members of the household.
I used to attempt the piano scores of my favourite oratorios, as
well as the simpler works of the chief classical composers. I was
also fond of browsing among my father's books and read om-
nivorously—almost anything from Bunyan's *Holy War* to
Whitaker's *Almanac*. But my scope was enlarged by the fact that

the nineties of last century saw a great development of public libraries; and about the time that I became a pupil at Henderson's one was opened in our suburb. My father was greatly interested in the movement and became chairman of the local library committee. Thus I had every encouragement to make the most of the opportunities provided and I certainly availed myself of them. The standard authors did not interest me much—Scott I found intolerably tedious, and Dickens, except as a humorist, was beyond me. It was at a much later stage that I learnt to appreciate Thackeray. But in my early 'teens I was a great admirer of G. H. Henty. All his works are concocted from the same formula. The central figure is a young man of outstanding ability, courage and intelligence, who goes through various adventures and always emerges successfully. The only difference between one story and another is in the setting. This may range from Ancient Egypt in *The Cat of Bubastes*, or pre-Saxon England in *Beric the Briton*, to *With Clive in India* or *Through Russian Snows*, or to *Young Franc-Tireurs* which brought one down to the Franco-Prussian War.

It was during my "prep." school days that my literary education was supplemented by the learning by heart of a piece of rigmarole on the lines of Samuel Foote's "incoherent story", which begins "She went into the garden to cut a cabbage leaf to make an apple pie". This composition, which was entitled Sir Gammer Vans, seems to have been handed down in my family, for I have never met anyone outside of it who had ever heard of this. I have also never seen any reference to it in print, and an inquiry in *Notes and Queries* elicited no replies. For this reason I take the opportunity of quoting this document in full, and if anyone who reads it can give me any information as to its origin, I should be most interested and grateful. It runs as follows:

> One Sunday morning, at about two o'clock on a weekday evening, as I was sailing over the mountains in my little boat, I met three men on horseback, riding on one donkey; and I asked them if they could tell me whether the little old woman was dead yet who was hanged last week for drowning herself in a shower of feathers. They said they could not

positively inform me, but that if I went to Sir Gammer Vans, he would tell me. "How shall I know his house?" said I. "Nothing could be easier," said they. "It's a brick house, built entirely of flint and stone, and standing alone amid twenty or thirty others exactly like it." "Nothing could be easier," I replied, and I went on my way. Now Sir Gammer Vans was a giant and a bottle-washer, and like all giants who are bottle washers he jumped out of a little thumb-bottle at the gate. "Good morning," says he. "Good morning," says I. "Will ye have breakfast with me?" says he. "With all my heart," says I. So he gave me a cup of cold veal and a slice of beer, and the little dog under the table licked up all the crumbs. "Hang him!" says I. "No, don't hang him," says he. "He killed a hare yesterday. If you don't believe me I'll show it you, alive and well in the basket." So he took me into the garden to show me his curiosities. In one corner there was an iron apple-tree entirely covered with pears and lead. In another, a fox hatching eagle's eggs. In the third, the hare which the dog had caught yesterday, alive and well in the basket. In the fourth, four and twenty hipper-switchers, threshing tobacco. They threshed so hard they drove the plug right through the wall and through a little dog running on the other side. I, hearing him howl, jumped over the wall and neatly turned him inside out. He ran away as if he hadn't an hour to live. Then I remembered that I had a warrant in my pocket to shoot venison for His Majesty's dinner. So I strung my arrow, poised my bow—when out flew a covey of partridges. Some say I killed twenty, but I'm sure I killed half a dozen, besides a dead salmon flying over the bridge, out of which I made the best apple-pie I ever tasted.

Another piece of family lore, which I remember and to which I have never seen any reference elsewhere, was a parody on *Hiawatha*. It went thus:

> He slew the mighty Mudjekeewis
> With its skin he made him mittens,
> Made them with the skinside outside,
> Made them with the furside inside.
> He, to get the skinside outside,
> Turned the furside (outside) inside.
> He, to get the furside inside,
> Turned the skinside (inside) outside.
> Thus he turned them outside inside.
> Thus he turned them inside outside.

It was while I was at Henderson's that I discovered the attraction of the *Boy's Own Paper*. I became a subscriber to it, and I

borrowed bound annual volumes from the public library. As a
magazine for boys it was extremely well edited, though it
tended perhaps to be a little "hearty" and improving, especially
in the "Answers to Correspondents". It had secured the services
of a number of first-class authors. There was, for example, Talbot
Baines Reed whose school stories—e.g. *The Fifth Form at St.
Dominic's* or *The Cock-House at Felsgarth*—are full of life and
vigour and interest, and deal with real schools and real boys—
a complete contrast to that sickening "wet" *Eric*. Ballantyne,
who was the chief purveyor of boys' adventure stories in my
youth, never appealed to me much, though he also contributed
occasionally to the *B.O.P.* Another author whom I could never
stomach was Dr. Gordon Stables, R.N., who specialised on tedious Scottish boys who wore kilts and were as hard as nails. I
suspect that he was also responsible for much of the "Answers to
Correspondents", in which readers were exhorted to take cold
baths and avoid "bad habits". More to my taste were the writings
of the Revd. A. N. Malan, who had a pretty wit and used
it effectively in describing the goings-on at Dr. Porchester's
Academy for Young Gentlemen.

My chief and lasting enthusiasm, however, was for the works
of Jules Verne. He was a frequent contributor to the *B.O.P.* and
some of his best known works first appeared in English in its
pages. It was there that I read with avidity *The Clipper of the
Clouds*, *The Giant Raft*, *The Castle of the Carpathians*, and many
more. That sent me to the public library where I discovered such
masterpieces as *Twenty-thousand Leagues under the Sea*, *Five Weeks
in a Balloon*, *From the Earth to the Moon*. I have found a continued
enjoyment in these and similar works, for they have an appeal to
boys of all ages. To my mind, however, Jules Verne's masterpiece
is *The Mysterious Island*—a work which, for some reason or
other, seems little known nowadays. It is in essence an application
of the educational theories of Herbert Spencer to the story of
Robinson Crusoe. The main plot is roughly as follows: During
the American Civil War five men and their dog escape by balloon
from the town of Richmond, Virginia. They are blown 7000

miles by a tempest and make a landfall on an unknown island; but in so doing they have to sacrifice the car of the balloon and its contents. Thus, unlike the original Robinson Crusoe, they have no convenient wreck from which to salvage the resources of civilisation. All they possess is their clothes, a couple of watches and a single match. It is a nervous moment when the match is utilised to start a fire. At first their only food is shell-fish, but snares are contrived out of a tough creeper in order to trap birds. The underlying purpose of the book is to show how one of the balloonists, Cyrus Smith, an engineer and a scientist, uses his knowledge in order to overcome all the difficulties of the situation. Man, if he has the right sort of practical education, can become master of his fate. It is a variation on the Spencerian theme: "What knowledge is of most worth? The uniform reply is Science." The latitude and longitude of the island are calculated with the aid of a watch and the altitude of the Southern Cross. Not only are bricks and earthenware vessels manufactured, but coal and iron-ore are discovered, and thus the metal is smelted and all kinds of tools and implements are made. From the chemicals found on the island in their raw state sulphuric and nitric acid are prepared; and nitro-glycerine becomes available for blasting rocks. A hole is blown in the side of a lake so that the water-level is lowered and access is gained to a cavern through which the outlet to the sea had originally flowed. Here the adventurers are installed, and Granite House—as their home is called—rapidly becomes fitted up with all modern conveniences. Water, for example, is laid on by directing a stream into Granite House. The efforts of Cyrus Smith and his companions to help themselves are rewarded by having a chest washed up on the shore. It contains a variety of tools, a supply of arms and ammunition, some instruments and utensils, clothes and books. Whence it comes is part of the mystery which is so skilfully interwoven in the narrative and which lends so much interest to it. Thus the range of possible activities is extended. A lift, worked by water-power, is installed; a bridge, a boat and a windmill are constructed. Finally Granite House is connected with a "corral", where the flocks are kept, by an electric telegraph contrived by Cyrus Smith. In fact there is no limit to what scientific knowledge and resource can do even on a desert island.

The works of Jules Verne, and *The Mysterious Island* in particular, directed my attention to a department of my education which had hitherto been entirely neglected. They helped me to realise the wonders of modern science and the possibilities of scientific invention. It is indeed remarkable that this author, whose *floruit* period was from about 1865 to 1875, should have anticipated in his romances many of the scientific achievements of the twentieth century. He forecast the submarine, he predicted that flying would be achieved by heavier-than-air machines, he even adumbrated space-travel—not, indeed, by means of rockets but by projectile fired from an immense cannon. But it was only from chance sources such as these that I got my ideas of what science was doing and possibly could do. No kind of instruction in this subject—or even in nature study—was given at any of the schools which I had attended hitherto. However, as I have said, even in the Thornton Heath days I had derived great pleasure from browsing at home in *Discoveries and Inventions of the Nineteenth Century*; and later I found in my father's library an ancient copy of a work on "Natural Philosophy" by the erratic Dionysius Lardner, as well as a book called *The Animal Creation* and Sir Robert Ball's *Star-Land*. All these had plenty of illustrations and were a perpetual source of interest.

An actual example of scientific achievement at the end of the nineteenth century was afforded by the erection in 1895 at Earl's Court of the "Great Wheel" to which I paid several visits. At the Chicago "World's Fair" Exhibition in 1893 a huge vertical wheel had been constructed by an engineer named Ferris. All round its periphery were slung passenger cars, so that as the wheel revolved one was treated to a circular trip in the air. The venture was so successful that the Ferris Wheel was reproduced on a larger scale at the Earl's Court Oriental Exhibition two years later. The London "Great Wheel" had a diameter of 300 feet. One could not only make the "round trip", which

took—so far as I remember—about three-quarters of an hour
with five or six stops, but it was also possible to ascend by a lift
to the top of the towers on which the axle-pivots rested, and
even to walk through the hollow axle itself. As the wheel went
round its motion was hardly perceptible, and one glided through
the air as if in a balloon. Just occasionally the mechanism would
get stuck, and then the passengers would be imprisoned in mid-
air until it started again. From the top stages of the journey an
extensive view over London and its environs could be obtained;
Windsor Castle for example, was clearly visible. Another *fin de
siècle* project which interested me greatly was the Wembley
Tower. Sir Edward Watkin, a railway magnate, sponsored a
scheme for constructing in Wembley Park, near Harrow, a huge
iron tower, destined to eclipse in size and height even M. Eiffel's
erection at the Paris Exhibition of 1889. But it had barely reached
the first stage when the work was abandoned. The Wembley
Tower remained an eye-sore for some years and was eventually
taken down. The Great Wheel, though a more successful venture,
was also dismantled. Replicas on a smaller scale of both Wheel and
Tower were afterwards erected at Blackpool.

There were few boys who could resist the fascination of a
steam-engine, and particularly of a locomotive. In the Thornton
Heath days one of our favourite occupations had been "playing
at trains". One ran along the edge of the pavement, moving one's
arms in imitation of cranks and connecting-rods, and emitting
puffing noises and an occasional whistle. From time to time one
would slow down, stop and move backwards, thus simulating
shunting. So I early became a railway enthusiast; and as I grew
older I amassed a quantity of technical information, so that I
could speak with authority about "Stirling singles" or "Webb
compounds" or "Stroudley 4–2–0's". The monthly issues of the
*Railway Magazine*, which I read with avidity at the public
library, were a mine of information on these subjects. Those
were certainly halcyon days for "loco-spotters". The railways at
this epoch, of course, had not yet been nationalised. There were
many different railways owned by private companies up and

down the country, and each company had its own special live and its distinctive types of locomotive. My earliest association had been with the London, Brighton, and South Coast Railway which ran through Thornton Heath. Its engines were painted a bright orange-yellow and were kept in spotless condition. On the top of the funnel there was always a flared and highly polished copper rim, which gave the finishing touch to the locomotive's handsome appearance. This railway also had the pleasing custom of giving its engines both a name and a number, and of painting the driver's name inside the cab; so that the collection of these data in a notebook was a hobby of perennial interest. When we removed to Suburbia my attention was transferred to the London and North Western Railway, with its "Jumbo's", like the famous *Charles Dickens*, and its "Compounds", like the equally famous *Jeanie Deans*. Not far away one could watch Midland locomotives which, together with their rolling stock, were painted a vivid red colour. They were built on graceful lines and had a flashing brass cover over the safety-valve. Every holiday provided a welcome opportunity to make the acquaintance of new types—the black and rather uninteresting London, Chatham and Dovers; the grass-green domeless South Easterns, with the safety-valve set in the middle of the boiler; the apple-green London and South Western engines and their hideous coaches with salmon-pink panels, which took us to Bishops Waltham. To one who can remember these things and who has retained a lifelong interest in them it is sad to think that the days of the steam locomotive have been numbered and that it has been re-placed by diesel or electric engines. A locomotive, with its *panache* of white steam, as it stood at the head of the train waiting for the signal to start, was like a horse straining at the leash. It was no longer a mere piece of machinery, but a living thing.

CHAPTER 8

# Cats and Other Interests

ALL my life I have been extremely fond of cats and have greatly valued their friendship and companionship. I am much less attracted to dogs. In my early days at Thornton Heath we did for a short time possess a collie named Shep; but he developed an embarrassing habit of bringing home unauthorised joints of meat from the butcher's shop opposite the pond, so that we had to get rid of him. Although I do not much like dogs as a class I have some good friends among individual dogs; but I dislike the habits of the type which is continually barking and "yapping", or jumping about and creating a disturbance. I am also revolted by the behaviour of dogs in the streets. The cat is by comparison a gentleman in his sanitary habits and his care for his personal appearance. If you give a saucer of milk to a poor, bedraggled stray cat, his first act after finishing it will be to start trying to tidy himself up. Cats can certainly make themselves a nuisance and the custom of "putting the cat out last thing" is not only unkind to the cat, but is also likely to disturb the neighbours. A German friend who was once staying with us remarked at breakfast time "There was a cat-music last night. I was woked." In order to avoid any possibility of caterwauling pussy should sleep at night in a basket (in my family it was always called a "bice"), and in a warm and draught-free place—preferably the kitchen. But personally I dislike the idea of pets (even cats) being allowed to sleep on their owner's bed.

My first interest in cats and their habits and characteristics was excited by a fine tabby kitten who became a member of our household when I was nearly 6. At the time a sister of my mother's "companion" was staying with us. She had married a Swedish army doctor, and had become so much naturalised in her adopted country that she lost to some extent the command of her native English. She was, by the way, the first woman I had ever seen smoking a cigarette. In those days and in my sector of society such a practice was utterly "taboo" for any "respectable" woman. I have referred to this lady because she was responsible for naming our new puss. He was called Putte (two syllables), which is apparently a Swedish slang term meaning "little chap". He was the precursor of a long line of feline companions. T. S. Eliot in his inimitable *Old Possum's Book of Practical Cats* has discussed at length the question of naming cats, and it is Michael Joseph, I think, who has said that the attitude of a cat-owner to his pet can to a large extent be estimated by the name he gives to it. Something obvious and unimaginative like Nigger or Ginger or Tiddles suggests that the cat's master or mistress is not really interested in him and considers him primarily as a mouse-catcher or a plaything. We may not go as far as T. S. Eliot who has suggested such dignified and peculiar appellations as Quaxo, Mundustrap, Coriocopat, Bombolurina and Jellylorum. But the cat who is regarded as a personality to be treated with respect, if not with affection, will be given a title appropriate to his standing. Dr. Johnson's cat, for whom he used to provide oysters, was called Hodge. Jeremy Bentham had a cat called Langborne. After a while he was promoted to become Sir John Langborne, and finally in his old age he took holy orders and was known as the Reverend Dr. John Langborne.

In my own case, Putte was succeeded by Bevis because I was reading some of Tennyson's *Idylls of the King* at my preparatory school at the time. Then in due course came Paul who arrived, already so called, as a gift from our doctor's wife—she bred pedigree cats. Later on, in my early married days, we had a black cat called Bub. He was so named by my wife because when I was at Oxford some of my friends used to call me Bub. It was said to

A bathing scene in the 1890's (see page 29).

General view of the Great Wheel at Earl's Court, 1898 (see page 68).

At the time of the Diamond Jubilee (1897) the London & North Western Railway painted three of its most up-to-date locomotives red, white and blue, respectively. This picture shows the white one, named "Queen Empress" (see page 70).

University College School, Gower Street (see page 87).

U.C.S. The new buildings from the north (see page 113).

be short for Beelzebub, but I am sure that this was a case of "Lucus a non Lucendo". Other family cats were Orlando who, like Katherine Hale's famous puss, was of the "marmalade" variety. Then came James, because he arrived on St. James' Day and finally Dinah, a she-cat who got her name from the mother of Alice in Wonderland's kittens. Other cats I have known included Doodle—a stray who arrived during a "doodle-bug" raid in the last war—Balkis ("I am black, but comely"), Percy ("because he can purr-see?"), and Nonny, which was short for "anonymous" because his owners could not think of something appropriate.

In my younger days it was not uncommon for little girls to be given the pet name "Pussy". Queen Victoria's eldest daughter, the Princess Royal, was christened Victoria Adelaide Mary Louise, but in the Queen's correspondence she is always referred to as "Pussy", and this is obviously what she was called by her family. Anyway, it is a pleasing and pretty word, and somehow is particularly applicable to cats because it seems to sum up the comfortable cosiness of the domestic cat in front of the fire or the elegant playfulness of the kitten with a piece of string or a ping-pong ball.

My close acquaintance with Alice in Wonderland was probably the reason why I made an attempt while I was at Henderson's to write a story on somewhat similar lines, entitled *Jane's Visit to Puss-catland*. Many years afterwards I rewrote it for the benefit of my daughter when she was a little girl. Jane is woken up at night by her cat Bevis who provides her with a fur suit which fits exactly and turns her into a veritable puss-cat. They scramble up on to the roof where there is an albatross waiting to take them away to Puss-catland. There Jane has many adventures, and in my account there was a good deal of imitation of Lewis Carroll's habit of playing with words. For example, the usual greeting was "good mousing". At the cat restaurant which Jane and Bevis visited the fare provided included Morelick's Milk and Miced Drinks. One chapter dealt with a visit to a kittens' school (a "kittengarten"), presided over by a dignified long-haired cat called Miss Muff—the Head Mewstress. When Jane and Bevis arrived a geography lesson was being given on Purrsia—a country governed by a ruler called the Chat (pronounced "Shah"). Although on the map it is nowadays called Iran, one can still see the Purrsian Cat in the atlas. The shape of the country closely resembles that of a recumbent cat. The two ears stick up just south of the Caucasus mountains and the town of Tabriz occupies one of the eyes. Pussy's back stretches along the south of the Caspian (?Catsian) Sea, and her hind quarters curve round to the east of this. One of her paws protrudes a little towards Baghdad in Iraq and she is obviously resting on a cushion north of the Persian Gulf and the Gulf of Oman. It is all quite life-like, and I hope that no political or military complication will ever blur the outline of Purrsia's Puss-catland.

I was always on good terms with the family cat and used to enjoy playing with her; but I had several other recreational interests as well. Like most boys today no less than in my "special period" I was greatly interested in philately. It was soon after I went to Henderson's that I began to collect stamps and I gradually amassed a quite considerable collection. My elders were laid under contribution—especially those who had correspondents in foreign parts; and I also had a source of supply in "swops" with my schoolfellows. It was our custom in addition to obtain quite a few specimens from "approval sheets" which were supplied by a firm in London. These sheets contained a variety of stamps, each of them priced, and a good proportion of our slender pocket-money (only a few pence a week) was periodically despatched to Messrs. Errington and Martin, as I believe the firm was called. It was easier to secure complete sets of stamps in those days than it has become since because there were so much fewer of them and they were not issued so frequently. The vogue for commemoratives was started by New South Wales in 1888 with a set to celebrate the centenary of the founding of the Colony. I managed to get the whole of it, including the 5/- and £1 values. This was followed by the famous Columbus issue of the United States, which commemorated the four-hundredth anniversary of the discovery of America. The custom of issuing commemorative and often highly artistic postage-stamps has spread enormously since my young days, and it is now, I suspect, a source of revenue to the countries concerned, because these stamps are not merely used for postage but are also bought in large quantities by dealers and collectors. Great Britain was late in the field in this respect, but we now seem to have adopted the practice with almost as much enthusiasm as the U.S.A. (a particular offender) or any other country. But it is not only governments which have benefited from philatelic enthusiasm. Between 1890 and 1898 some of the stamp issues of certain Central American states were printed in the United States by a speculator named N. F. Seebeck. He secured the right to use the plates in order to make reprints to be sold again to stamp dealers and collectors. The result is that in such cases the postally used stamp has a higher market value than the unused variety—the opposite of what usually happens. However, I welcomed whatever I could get. If I still possessed my youthful collection it would probably be really valuable, for I had a good variety of quite early issues; but later on, when other enthusiasms prevailed, I sold it for a mere song after hawking it round several stamp-dealers in London.

About the time that I started to collect stamps I acquired another enthusiasm—toy trains. These were not of the sophisticated type that are associated with the name of Hornby and which run on rails and are operated by clock-work or electricity. We played with our trains on the floor and manipulated them by hand. All the same, they were pretty good replicas of the real thing, though I suspect that they hailed from America. The carriages were "cars" of the type used on the Canadian Pacific Railway and which were illustrated in my *Discoveries and Inventions of the Nineteenth Century*. The locomotives were furnished with cow-catchers and had plate-shaped spark-catchers on the top of their funnels. All this led to the invention of an imaginary railway which used this rolling-stock. I drew maps of it which I still possess and had great fun in making up the names of the stations. The line started from Petershed and ended at the appropriately named town of Terminster. Here are one or two of the places *en route*—the names are taken at random: Shepford, Hith and Frayfield, Hackhurst, Runmouth, Aldrington, Chipping Wetham. There were 321 stations like this on the line and they were shown not only on the map, but also in lists giving their distance from Petershed. On the back of one of the maps are plans of the principal main-line stations. There are also some drawings of the locomotives used on the line and these are obviously copied from the toy engines themselves. Appended information states that "total length of engine and tender over buffers is 47′ 6″—total hight (*sic*) from rail to funnel is 13′ 3‴". There is also a section of the locomotive showing the tubular boiler and the valve-gear. The influence of the *Railway Magazine* (see p. 69) is very much in evidence.

When I was about 13 this railway enthusiasm was stimulated by an actual steam-driven model locomotive which some kind relative had given me. It was made entirely of brass and had two oscillating cylinders to drive the wheels. The heat required for raising steam was provided by a lamp under the boiler, fed by a small tank containing methylated spirit. This engine did not run on rails, but, like my toy trains, it could be used on the floor so long as this was not provided with carpets. One of the most satisfying accessories of my steam engine was the whistle. A less exciting toy of a similar kind was a stationary engine also operated by steam. It had an upright boiler and one cylinder which worked on to a wheel. I suppose steam toys of this kind have now been superseded by electrical ones.

Yet another interest was the collecting of leaden soldiers. They were contrived so as to be hollow and were not at all heavy. They were very exact replicas of the real thing. The infantry were resplendent in scarlet coats with all the correct facings, and they wore the regulation dome-shaped helmets. One could get them in various positions—marching with shouldered arms or standing with fixed bayonets for repelling a charge. The cavalry were provided with gleaming swords made of tiny slips of tin. These military toys were manufactured by a firm with the appropriate name of Brittain. As in the case of my trains, I managed to provide a sort of background to the actual toys themselves. Underneath the stand of each soldier I scratched a number and a list was then made in a notebook (I still possess this also). Every soldier was given a name—the sergeant, for example, complete with crimson sash, was for some reason or other christened Alan Binnie.

I have often heard objections raised to letting children play with toy soldiers or toy weapons, on the grounds that it tends to inculcate a militaristic outlook and ideas of military "glory", and to obscure the real meaning of armaments and all that they stand for. Nowadays these manifestations seem to be associated not so much with soldiers themselves but rather with cowboys and their accoutrements and with "western" films. Miniature mechanised contrivances, such as tanks and artillery, also seem popular. But I doubt how far such devices really encourage militarism and I think boys soon outgrow this stage. Judging by my own case, I am sure that playing with soldiers did not in any way encourage me to aim at a career in the army or stimulate admiration for military glamour. As Stanley Hall says, boys of about 11 to 15 tend to imitate "social units characteristic of the lower stages of human evolution", and he instances "pirates, robbers and soldiers".

Another new interest: it was while I was on holiday at Sandgate near Folkestone, somewhere about the year 1897, that I had my first ride in a motor vehicle. It was what we should now call a motor-coach and a service had been started to ply between Folkestone and Hythe. But the first private motor that I can remember was introduced a year or two later by our family doctor. This was rather like a couple of wide armchairs, mounted on a chassis. In front there was a long bonnet flanked by two large and imposing brass lamps. There were no electric sparking-plugs, but there was a wick-type carburettor which had to be replenished with petrol at frequent intervals. It was reported also that in this particular model the orifice of the pipe leading from the tank to the engine was slightly above the bottom of the tank, so that when the supply of petrol was very low it was unable to run out. To remedy this, when the doctor came to a hill it was said that he had to reverse and go up backwards. This had the effect of tipping the petrol so that its level came above the outlet of the pipe.

The lot of the motorist in those days was not an easy one. The Locomotives on Highways Act of 1896 permitted "light locomotives" to use the roads, but speed was limited to 14 miles per hour. Hitherto the maximum permitted speed had been only 4 miles per hour and the vehicle had to be preceded by a man carrying a red flag. I suppose that regulation was devised with steam-rollers in view. However, the Act of 1896 was celebrated by a huge motor parade from London to Brighton in which fifty-four cars of various types took part. The event was com-memorated by a popular song which was adapted to the tune of *Funiculi, Funicula*. I can remember only part of it:

> ... People shouted "They don't know where they are!"
> They laughed at me, they laughed at Ma,
> They laughed at Sue, they laughed at Pa,
> When we went to Brighton on our famous motor car.

The parade has since become an annual event and an opportunity for vintage cars to display their prowess.

CHAPTER 9

# The Chrestomathic School

IT SEEMS obvious that the members of my family originally belonged to the English Church, because from time to time we produced a parson. Examples are the Cambridge vicar in the seventeenth century, to whom reference has already been made, and another ancestor who was incumbent of the village of Barrington. My great-great-grandfather Edward (second of that name) married Mary Boosey (her family are today concerned with music publishing) on January 18th, 1791; and according to the family Bible the ceremony took place at (old) St. Pancras Church. That fact may possibly argue membership of the Establishment. But the newly married couple afterwards became associated with a small and exclusive dissenting sect called Sandemanians or Glassites. This had originally come from Scotland and the founder, John Glass, had been a minister of the Established Kirk. Under the influence of his disciple, Robert Sandeman, the society developed, though it can never have been numerous. It was strongly evangelical and anti-Erastian; it believed in justification by faith and it held a weekly celebration of the Holy Communion—or was it the Agape?

Sandemanians are perhaps still remembered because Michael Faraday, in spite of his eminence as a scientist, was a faithful adherent of their strict and even narrow-minded sect. Thus it came about that my great-grandfather's sister Sarah in 1821 became Mrs. Faraday. Her father (the Edward already referred to) was an elder in the Sandemanian meeting which the great scientist attended. Five years later his son John (who, like his father, was a liveryman of the Goldsmiths' Company) married Faraday's sister Margaret; and in subsequent generations there were several alliances between the two families. For example, my great-uncle Frederick, the artist, married Alice Faraday who was the scientist's niece. For these reasons "great uncle Faraday" was always regarded (not quite justly) as a family possession. He died as far back as 1867, but my father remembered him well and possessed copies of *On the Various Forces of Matter* and *The Chemical History of a Candle* which had been presented to him by the great man himself. He also, as a small boy, used to visit the Faradays in the house near Hampton Court which had been put at their disposal by Queen Victoria. My only connection with Michael Faraday was through my grandfather's cousin Jane. She had been the scientist's favourite niece and had lived with the Faradays at Hampton Court. She survived until 1911, and I can remember being taken to see her—an old lady in a grey dress and a lace cap, with a large tabby cat on her lap. But what chiefly impressed me was a model of a lighthouse lantern which had originally been made for Faraday when he was scientific adviser to Trinity House, and which had come into her possession. It was a model of the lantern of the Upper South Foreland lighthouse where I believe electricity was used as an illuminant for such purpose for the first time in England. The model was made of brass with thick glass lenses. At the bottom was a small handle; but however quickly one turned this the lantern itself revolved with the most exasperating slowness.

Although the family allegiance to Sandemanianism did not persist, my paternal grandfather was a staunch nonconformist and a deacon of the Cross Street Chapel, Islington. My mother's father held a similar position in a Congregational church. But these traditions tended to pass me by. During my early days at Thornton Heath my religious training (such as it was) remained in the hands of my governesses. My father's theory, apparently, was that children should be given no religious instruction, but should be allowed in due course to make their own investigations and come to their own decisions. I could not be taken to the Congregational church, which my grandfather attended, because this was situated at Selhurst, some distance from our house. I suppose it would have been considered hardly less than sinful to have the "barouche" out on Sunday. So when I did go to church I was taken to the local representative of the Establishment, where a service of evangelical and Simeonite austerity was provided—a rather boring performance for a small boy. A branch of my grandmother's family were Roman Catholics. One of her brothers was a benefactor of the Benedictine monastery at Ramsgate; and in the garden of his house at Broadstairs he had a small chapel erected so that Mass could be made available for the faithful who lived in or near the town. Thus I inherited a confused religious tradition ranging from convinced nonconformity through indifferentism and dilute Anglicanism to distant rumours of Roman Catholicism.

When we migrated to Suburbia I went regularly with my step-mother to an English Church, where at any rate I used to get some fun by trying to sing alto in the hymns. After a year or two at Henderson's, perhaps owing to the Scottish influences to which I have referred, I migrated to the Presbyterian Church. There I was introduced to the linguistic eccentricities of the metrical psalms,* to long and philosophical sermons, and to extempore prayers delivered with unction and a thick Scottish accent. The Presbyterians seemed to be particularly bitter against Roman Catholicism. I still remember a sermon in which the preacher told us how, during a holiday in Italy, he had attended a service at St. Peter's, Rome. "I wurrshipped", he said "—weeth deeficulty." A Scottish friend of mine not long ago said that he suspected that the pagan festival of Hogmanay was celebrated in Scotland in preference to the commemoration of our Lord's birth at Christmas simply because the feast of the Nativity was

---

* For example: In order none can reckon them
　　　　　　　To Thee if them declare
　　　　　　　And speak of them I would they more
　　　　　　　Than can be numbered are.　(See Psalm xl. 5.)

associated with Catholicism. This, of course, may or may not be true. But I was never really attracted by the Presbyterian outlook or form of service. It seemed strange to have no room in the pews to kneel down, as I had always been taught to do. There were references to kneeling in the hymns which were sung, but the actual practice was an uncomfortable crouch involving compression of the abdomen. Most nonconformist churches, and many English ones too, depended largely on pew-rents. For an annual payment one secured a reserved seat in the house of God, but the poorer members of the flock and mere visitors were relegated to the "free seats" at the back of the church. It seems a distasteful system, but I suppose churches cannot exist without funds and this is one method of ensuring an income.

But what I found most tedious in the Presbyterian service was the prayers. It was difficult to accustom oneself to having to listen to what Mr. McTavish or Dr. McPherson had to say to the Almighty. A good part of their extemporisations consisted of clichés or quotations from the Bible. Later, when I was at Oxford, one of my chief friends was the son of a Wesleyan minister. I spent an Easter vacation with the family at their manse in Northumberland. After breakfast every morning it was the custom to have "family prayers". This is a practice that was by no means uncommon in my youth and it was certainly not confined to clerical households; but it seems to have died out nowadays. The chief feature of our devotions was a prayer offered by the minister himself. It was a little embarrassing to be referred to directly as "the stranger within our gates" or "the sojourner in our midst". My friend, however, had from long experience sized up his father's technique. He would say to me "Today will be the turn of 'may our great men be good men', and we shall have a reference to 'the cattle upon a thousand hills'." If his forecast proved correct I was committed to giving him a cigarette; but if the predicted phrase did not appear, my friend gave me one. It was remarkable how often his surmise was justified, and I am sure that his score was at least equal to mine. Anyhow, even in my early teens I preferred the dignified anonymity of the Book of

Common Prayer; but as regards these practices much obviously depends upon what one has got used to. There are many who find the liturgy of the English Church formalistic, and its ritual a hindrance rather than a help to worship. In religion, as in other matters, "de gustibus non est disputandum".

Yet another influence which dates from my suburban days: In his *English Social History* (p. 571) G. M. Trevelyan points out that "When Queen Victoria died drinking was still a great evil from the top to the bottom of society," and he comments that "Gambling perhaps now does more harm than drink." When I was a boy it was no uncommon sight to see a drunken man staggering about the street, and in contemporary issues of *Punch*—especially in the drawings of Charles Keane—he often appeared as a supposed figure of fun, in spite of what he really was—a tragic character. The average public-house in a city was usually a sordid kind of place frequented by the "lower classes". It was not inaptly termed a "gin palace". All this helps to explain the so-called "Temperance" movement which was particularly strong perhaps in nonconformist circles. Even children were proselytised. While I was at Henderson's I was induced to join a branch of the "Young Abstainers' Union", which was attached to the Presbyterian Church. It held improving meetings periodically and at these we wore blue ribbon badges to show our adherence to the movement.

I have tended since those days to resent the application of the term "Temperance" to the practice of teetotalism or total abstinence from alcoholic drinks of any kind. Such an extreme is no more temperate than the abuse of such stimulants. There is surely a *via media*, and the best public-house sign I have ever seen is *The Moderation*. It is curious that sincerely religious people, many of whom believed in the verbal inspiration of the Bible, should have supported such a movement. Our Lord's first miracle was designed to encourage the festivities at a wedding by turning water into wine; and the most solemn and sacred ceremony of the Christian Church is concerned with the consecration of the symbolic cup which was given with the instruction "Drink ye all of this". The English translation is ambiguous, but the original Greek makes it clear that the word "all" refers to "ye". Moreover, the rite was to be repeated "as oft as ye shall drink it".

My connection with Presbyterianism was a passing phase, and before long I reverted to the English Church and eventually I was confirmed—appropriately enough—in St. Paul's Cathedral and by the Bishop of London, Dr. Winnington-Ingram. What he said in his address I have completely forgotten, but as I had hitherto not had much experience of cathedral services I was enormously impressed by the singing of the choir. There is nothing more heavenly among earthly sounds than a well-trained boy's voice; and whatever criticisms may be made of the behaviour of choir-boys it is surely fitting that the praises of the Church should be led by children. "Ex ore infantium perfecisti laudem." One other thing remains indelible in my memory. During the actual laying-on of hands the hymn "Come, Holy Ghost" was sung. As the number of candidates was very large, the organist—Sir George Martin—extemporised for a little while between each of the verses. Every time he took the Attwood tune, but treated it in a different way. For me it was a most uplifting experience. I have often been reminded of it by a passage in one of E. F. Benson's novels, referring to a Holy Communion service in St. Paul's: "Between the verses the organ always played a little symphony, gathering together the melody. The organ was like some devout spirit thinking over what had been sung."

Such then, in outline, was my religious education—so far as it went. But with the nonconformist outlook of my grandparents there went also a strong political tradition—a tradition of liberalism. Mr. Gladstone's was a name to conjure with in our family. He was indeed the "Grand Old Man" (G.O.M.), and was the object of adulation and admiration such as has been accorded to Sir Winston Churchill in our own day. From time to time Mr. Gladstone used to stay with Lord and Lady Aberdeen at Dollis Hill House; and on Sundays he would go over to Old Willesden Church and read the lessons at the morning service. On one occasion my father took me to hear and see the great man. As we came out of the church he said to me "You will remember this all your life"—and as a matter of fact he was quite right. All the same, in spite of the family tradition, as I have grown older I have come more and more to dislike party politics. There seems to me much to be said for the criticisms levelled at the party system by W. Gilbert in *Iolanthe*:

> When in that House M.P.'s divide
> If they've a brain and cerebellum too
> They've got to leave that brain outside
> And vote just as their leaders tell 'em to.

As an elderly charlady once remarked to me, "Members of Parliament—what are they after all? They're only prawns!"

The religious and political tradition which came from both my father's and my mother's sides of the family explains the choice of the school to which I was sent at the age of $13\frac{1}{2}$, when I left Henderson's. There was never any suggestion that I should go away to be a boarder. The public-school for day-boys most accessible from my home was St. Paul's, and I have sometimes regretted that I was not entered there. But although St. Paul's was associated with the Mercer's Company, it was a Church of England school and its headmaster was in Holy Orders. My family tradition lay in a different direction. A combination of nonconformity and liberal politics demanded an undenominational type of education in a "progressive" atmosphere; and this, it was thought, would be provided by the school of which my father, three of my uncles and various other members of the family had already been members—University College School. Although this institution had neither the antiquity nor the standing of St. Paul's, it had a history of peculiar interest. It could boast a long list of very distinguished old boys. But, apart from this, it stood for something quite definite and *sui generis*; and to explain what this was it is necessary to go back to the circumstances in which the School was founded.

Even at the beginning of the nineteenth century there were only two universities in England—Oxford and Cambridge. Their

traditions and their expensiveness made them accessible only to
the wealthy and leisured classes, while their close association with
the English Church meant that no dissenter could enjoy their full
privileges. There was a growing dissatisfaction with such a state
of things on the part of liberals, nonconformists, Jews, Roman
Catholics, secularists, men who were more interested in the new
sciences than in the old humanities, and the successful manu-
facturers and business magnates who believed in a "useful",
rather than a traditional, education. So the democratic and
utilitarian tendencies of the day allied themselves with the
scientific and secularist movements in providing an entirely new
institution of general and vocational education for the benefit
of those to whom Oxford and Cambridge were closed by reason
of religious tests or expense or unsuitability. In this way a college,
calling itself "London University", was founded in Gower Street
in 1828. It was a proprietary institution and it owed its inception
largely to the poet Thomas Campbell and the statesman Henry
Brougham. Amongst the Whigs and Radicals who sponsored the
new college were the utilitarian philosophers Jeremy Bentham
and James Mill, the educationist Birkbeck, the politician Joseph
Hume, and the historian George Grote. There were to be no tests
and theology was to be kept out of the curriculum. In order to
provide a *pépinière* of entrants to this university a school was
founded by certain of the proprietors—among them Henry
Brougham and James Mill; and it was given the name of "The
London University School". In 1836 an arrangement was made
by which the college in Gower Street and King's College—a
Church of England counterblast which had been opened in the
Strand in 1831—together with certain medical schools, could
submit students to be examined and given degrees by an independent body called "The University of London". This
necessitated renaming the institution in Gower Street "University
College, London"; and at the same time the school that was
associated with it became University College School—or, as it is
now more familiarly known in the sporting news, "U.C.S."
The tradition of religious toleration and catholicity of curriculum,

inherited from the College, has throughout been characteristic of the School; but it has grown less distinctive with the development of similar features in other well-known schools. It can at least be said that U.C.S. was a pioneer in this direction.

At the start the School was accommodated in a house in Gower Street, but it was soon moved into the College itself; and when the south wing was built in three stages between 1860 and 1876 this was occupied by the School. There it remained until 1907 when it was transferred to new buildings at Hampstead. There were four floors and on each there was an internal corridor, like a dark tunnel even on a bright day, because it had no direct light from outside. In the basement there were cloak-rooms, a refreshment room with a tuck-shop, a dining-room where (according to the prospectus) one could obtain a dinner "price one shilling and twopence (exclusive of beer)". On the other three floors the class-rooms opened off the corridors on either side, and each had the name of an English or Greek letter. There were also a staff-room, a monitor's room, and an office presided over by the Registrar. It was from him that one purchased textbooks and other necessary gear. There was no school hall, but we had the use of the Botanical Theatre, which was really part of the College, though access to it was gained by a staircase from the School playground.

Just beyond this there was a spacious and well-fitted gymnasium, which was said to be the best thing of its kind in London. Here I spent many happy hours, for although physical education formed no part of the regular curriculum I took gymnastics as an "extra". The emphasis, however, was rather on display than development. We did various exercises on the parallel bars and vaulting horse; but my favourite was the horizontal bar on which I eventually learnt to do the "hock swing round" and other spectacular feats. I suppose that this was the reason why I was included in the school team which used to give a display on speech day—and was afterwards allowed to clear up all that remained of the refreshments. It was a glorious mixed feast of iced coffee, lemonade, meringues, jellies, cakes and sandwiches of all kinds, to which we did full justice. At one side of the gymnasium some fives-courts were provided. On the south side of the school building there was a large gravelled playground, and one corner of it was paved. Here the cricket experts used to practise. The greatest feat of all was to make so mighty a swipe as to send the ball on to the top of the school building, or even over into the College quadrangle. This was, I believe, actually achieved by one of my contemporaries who afterwards gained a "blue" at Cambridge for association football, although he came from a "rugger" school.

The provision of playing-fields for a school situated in the heart of London was a more difficult matter. When I first went to U.C.S. in 1897 we used to travel out by the old Metropolitan Railway to a ground at Willesden Green. But in 1900 a large playing-field was purchased at Neasden and a palatial pavilion was erected there. It gave us plenty of space for cricket in summer and rugby football in winter. For reasons which I have already given I did not take part in the former game; but, though never in the least expert, I managed to get much enjoyment from the latter. I was handicapped by lack of weight and by rather "rabbity" physique, but I made an attempt to learn the duties of a scrum half. I never got further than membership of a house team, but I have retained an interest in rugby football all my life. The only disadvantage of our Neasden playing-field was that it lay between a fever hospital and a tributary of the river Brent. At times the damp fog which settled on it was so dense that one could not see the goal-posts from the half-way line—a fact which added to the uncertainties of the game. The field has now disappeared owing to the construction of the North Circular Road.

I have always been glad that I went to a "rugger" school and so acquired an interest in this game, even though I was a very indifferent player. "Soccer" may doubtless afford opportunity for skill and sportsmanship, but I greatly dislike its "associations"— pools, hooliganism at matches, vandalism in railway trains, professionalism and commercialisation with its buying and selling of players by means of enormous transfer fees. All these things seem to me the antithesis of sportsmanship, and one can understand why so many schools nowadays prefer the Rugby code.

Jeremy Bentham, who—as has been said—was concerned in the foundation of University College, had adumbrated what he called a "Chrestomathic School". It was to teach what was "conductive to useful knowledge", corporal punishment was to be proscribed, careful records of pupils' progress were to be kept, and delinquences were to be registered in a "black book". Great emphasis was to be laid on the appropriate grouping of pupils in classes. "A Scholar", says Bentham, "belongs to *as many* classes, at the same *time*, as there are different *branches* in which he receives instruction; *put back* in one he may, at the same time, be *advanced* in another."\* As Professor Adamson points out, "University College School was in some respects a partial realisation of Bentham's Chrestomathic School".† Although, like most schools of its type, U.C.S. gave serious attention to the teaching of the classics, it was a pioneer in the broadening of the curriculum. As early as 1859 a laboratory had been fitted up for the teaching of practical chemistry. The School was also one of the first to give up Euclid and to teach geometry on modern lines. The reformed pronunciation of Latin was introduced in 1860. Again U.C.S. throughout has followed the Benthamite tradition in not resorting to the use of corporal punishment. If homework were unsatisfactory the culprit was given a square metal plate on which the room-letter was stamped. This was called a "T.B. ticket", and it had to be taken to the Registrar's office and exchanged for the "Task Book" in which the delinquent's name was entered, together with details of the returned work. This had to be repeated after school hours in the "T.B. room", under the supervision of the "T.B. master". It seems a rather elaborate procedure, but apparently it worked. For serious offences against school rules and for bad behaviour an entry was made in the "Appearing Book". This involved an interview with the Headmaster—though what transpired as the result of that I am unable to say

\* Jeremy Bentham, *Works* (1843), VIII, p. 52.
† *English Education, 1760–1902*, p. 104.

W.T.T.D.—D

because fortunately I never went through this experience. There was even a Benthamite "Black Book", too dreadful even to be imagined. I never heard of anybody being entered in this; I presume that it would have been a preliminary to expulsion. So, in spite of the fact that no use was made of the cane, the general discipline of the School was surprisingly good. The monitors, as the prefects were called, were completely responsible for order in the corridors and on the stairs. There was a hierarchy of these officials—a captain, a lieutenant, two sergeants and eight or ten ordinary monitors. One wore a silver badge in one's button-hole when one was on duty. New monitors were elected by the existing body; but there were always two who had been appointed directly by the Headmaster and who had seniority over those who had been co-opted. It was a proud day for me when I became a "headmaster's monitor".

Bentham had laid stress on the keeping of detailed school records of individual pupils—a recommendation which has quite a modern touch. Throughout the history of the School this practice had been customary. In my time an elaborate report was sent to one's parents every month. For each School subject it showed one's form, the number of boys in it, and one's form-order. Under each heading it also gave an assessment in three classes (1—"thoroughly satisfactory", 2—"fairly satisfactory", 3—"hardly satisfactory"), for conduct, diligence and progress. A more thorough scheme could hardly be devised. There was an entry to show how many times (if any) one had been late or absent. At the bottom were printed whatever notices from time to time were necessary for the information of parents. At the end of the summer and autumn terms, also, a booklet was published containing a complete "Honour List". It comprised notices to parents, a report of the speeches delivered on prize-day, a list of distinctions gained by Old Gowers, and class-lists for the whole school. Here again the letters C, H and V were used to show those boys who were commended, highly commended, and very highly commended; but these symbols were used with discretion. One did not get a V automatically if one were top of one's form;

nor was it necessary to attain this eminence in order to qualify for it. On the other hand, it was quite possible for a determined plodder, or a boy handicapped by absence, to be given a letter of commendation even if he happened to be low in form order. There must have been a great deal of thought and work behind all this.

A more definite adoption of Bentham's Chrestomathic theories was in the school organisation. This has been described as follows: "Summarily stated, the principle of the organisation of this school is that boys may be reclassified for every single subject of study, and it is possible for each boy to have a separate time-table—i.e. to pursue a combination of studies unlike that of any other boy."* As an illustration of this system I can quote from my own experience. When I first entered the School I was placed in the Upper IV for Latin, the Lower IV for Greek, the Upper II for French, the IV for English, History and Geography, the upper III for Arithmetic and the Lower III for Mathematics. The drawing up of time-tables such as these was the unenviable task of the Headmaster, Henry Weston Eve, during the summer holidays. As unfortunately his handwriting was completely illegible the resulting confusion which reigned in the School during the first few days of the Autumn term is more easily imagined than described.

* P. A. Barnett (ed.), *Teaching and Organisation*, p. 21.

## CHAPTER 10

# Early Days at U.C.S.

It was in September 1897 that I became a pupil at U.C.S. and I remained there for six years. In those days a large proportion of the boys came in by train from the suburbs, but there was always, of course, a walk from the terminus to the School. The neighbourhood of Bloomsbury and the Euston Road had in those days its special dangers for adolescents, and it was by no means unknown for older boys to be solicited in the streets on their way home in the evening. This matter gave the School authorities some anxiety, but I do not think that the problem ever became serious. Most of us were only too anxious to get to the railway station and catch the first train to our destination; but sometimes we stopped on the way to purchase a supply of roasted chestnuts. They were sold by a man with a barrow on which was a coke-fed stove. On top of this the chestnuts were cooked, so that they were always hot and tasty.

In my case going to school involved travelling to and from Euston on the London and North Western Railway, which was one of the most efficient of British lines. Even on our suburban trains the rolling-stock was comfortably fitted-up and kept in perfect order. For the long-distance expresses corridor coaches were beginning to be introduced in the last years of the nine-teenth century; but they were by no means universally employed. Some of the older carriages had "coupés"—single-sided compartments at the end of a coach, with windows opposite. I suppose that the intention was to attach them at the rear of a train, so that one could get a clear view of the receding landscape; but it usually happened that all one could see was the end of the next coach. Du Maurier once had a drawing in *Punch* depicting two newly married couples who had booked reserved compartments for their honeymoon journey. Unfortunately they were each provided with "coupés" at the ends of two carriages, facing one another. Not only was the introduction of corridors in its infancy, but the heating of railway carriages also left much to be desired. Systems of steam-heating began to be adopted at about the same time as corridors; but before that one had to rely on getting a "foot-warmer"—if one were lucky. This was a flat, metal box, about 3 feet long, hermetically sealed and containing some substance which retained heat. It was put on the floor of the compartment and helped to keep one's feet warm on a long journey, though it must have had a deleterious effect on the leather of one's shoes. However, on a short suburban journey such luxuries were unknown, and on our way to and from school we just sat in the cold. As for the lighting of railway carriages, gas was beginning to be used by some of the more go-ahead lines; but oil was still a quite usual illuminant. It was contained in cylindrical pots which stood in a row along the roof of the coach—one pot over each compartment. Reading during a journey after dark was almost impossible. The oil-lamps emitted a feeble glimmer; and under the light, at the bottom of the hemispherical glass shade, there was usually a pool of dirty water which swayed about with the motion of the train.

Becoming a season-ticket holder on the North Western Railway, therefore, brought a number of new interests; and I felt that it was something of a distinction to have left the local preparatory school and to have joined the not inconsiderable number of U.C.S. boys who travelled backwards and forwards to Euston. A daily railway journey to and from school may involve a waste of time and energy, but there are compensations and I do not think that I ever found such travelling irksome. In the morning we had to fit in with the army of business and professional men (most of them wearing frock-coats and top hats) who, like ourselves, went daily to their work in London. But in the afternoon, on the way back, we usually managed to get a compartment to ourselves. There was—as might be expected—a tendency to make the most of the occasion, and new boys had to undergo the ordeal of being put into the luggage-rack or under the seat; but on the whole I think we behaved ourselves pretty well. However, the North Western Company had a habit in those days of sticking paper labels (gummed only at the corners), marked SMOKING or LADIES ONLY or RESERVED, on the windows of certain compartments in the long-distance trains; and it was an act of fearful daring to nip in, before any of the passengers had arrived and when no porters were looking, and purloin the label. Some of us managed to form small collections of these trophies. On one occasion, however, a certain one of my companions (he eventually became an eminent surgeon and was knighted) was caught red-handed by a ticket-collector. He was taken summarily to a neighbouring stand-pipe and had his head held under a stream of cold water. Today such an incident would doubtless be followed by indignant letters of complaint from the parent to the railway company, and might even lead to legal proceedings—or, at any rate, to a psychological examination of the delinquent. But in this case everyone—including the victim—regarded the matter as a huge joke; and the hobby of label-collecting did not suffer any considerable diminution of popularity.

The Midland Railway at St. Pancras and the Great Northern at King's Cross also brought contingents to the School; but many boys also came by the Underground to Gower Street station, which is now called Euston Square. The contrast between conditions on this railway today and those which obtained in my youth almost beggar description. In the place of comfortable and airy electric trains (if one can disregard the overcrowding at rush hours) the Metropolitan and District companies employed steam locomotives which, in spite of special exhaust arrangements, filled the tunnels and stations with smoke and fumes and dirt. I am glad that I was spared having to travel daily under such mephitic conditions. Once, however, when we had been for an excursion up the river with a cousin who was suffering from a severe attack of hay-fever, he recovered immediately when we returned by Underground, though the atmosphere there choked the rest of us. On this railway the seats in the third-class compartments had no upholstery to mitigate their hardness. This was also the case on the North London Railway which had a terminus at Broad Street and ran through Canonbury; it was therefore a line on which I frequently travelled. There the third-class coaches were open from end to end, because the backs of the seats extended barely as high as one's shoulders. Sometimes the tedium of the journey would be enlivened by a travelling musician. Equipped with a kind of zither and two small hammers, he would give a short recital of popular tunes as the train rumbled on. Just before it reached the next station his cap would be passed round the carriage over the backs of the seats, then, pocketing the proceeds, he would dash out as soon as the train arrived, and repeat the whole performance in the next coach.

All these experiences increased the interest in railways and everything pertaining to them which I had formed at an earlier stage, and to which I have already referred. Every day there was something new to see and I was quite proud to be a regular traveller. I was also proud of my new school cap of black and cerise, with its acorn badge, and of the fact that I no longer carried my school-books in a satchel. Such an article was absolutely taboo at U.C.S. Instead one was equipped with a leather bag of ample proportions. A jeering board-school boy once, during a passage of arms, described mine as a "plum-pudding case"—surely a stroke of genius, though I am not quite sure what it means.

Life at my new school was very different from that at Henderson's. For example, one soon learnt to be utterly ashamed of possessing a Christian name. Even today I find it a little embarrassing to be expected to address acquaintances outside my immediate family in this way, and still more to receive the same familiarity from them. It is even more difficult to get reconciled to being called "dear" or "love" in shops or buses. Recently I held the door of a shop open for a good lady who acknowledged the action by saying "Ta, duck". Allergy to Christian names is a curious hangover from one's youth; but when I was at U.C.S. the very worst insult that one could offer a schoolfellow was to discover his Christian name and then hurl the opprobrious epithet at him. It was only girls who used such names! I gather that this was the usual contemporary attitude at schools of this type.*

In my early days at U.C.S. I was also a little overawed by the large number of boys (some of them young men), the size of the building, the high stone corridors, the dignified monitors controlling the traffic, the impressive school sergeant with his beribboned black uniform trimmed with gold—and not least by the variety of gowned masters to whom I went for the various classes to which I was assigned. The curious Benthamite system of regrouping boys for each separate subject meant that the form-master organisation in its ordinary sense was impossible. To rectify this deficiency there existed a number of what were called "consulting masters". These were senior members of staff and every boy was accredited to one or the other of them. Thus they stood in somewhat the same relationship to their "consults" as a housemaster in a boarding school does to the members of his house. They were rather like what in an Oxford college is called a "moral tutor". Each consulting master took a personal and particular interest in the boys for whom he was responsible, and the development of their characters and their progress in the school were matters of special concern to him. If one had difficulties it was to one's consulting master that one went for advice and help. As far as I remember the system worked extremely well and the masters concerned took their responsibilities seriously. Each consulting master's group was named from the letter of his class-room. For example, I was in *Theta*. Each group, therefore, corresponded exactly to the "House" in any modern day-school. It had its athletic teams and other forms of organised activity;

* See Harold Nicolson, *Good Behaviour*, p. 272.

and there was always keen rivalry between the different groups—particularly in house matches. The consulting-master groups have, I believe, in recent times been renamed "demes"—a happy association with a type of organisation in ancient Athens which furnishes a close parallel.

I was allocated to a certain "Charlie" Potter, who had been my father's consulting-master. His appearance was unkempt and his beard thin and straggly. But he had a twinkling eye and, although one of the most erratic and unsystematic people I have ever met, he took a real interest in his protégés. He was rather a joke in the school, but it was a good joke and not a malicious one. He never taught us much about the subject prescribed on the time-table; but we enjoyed his lessons partly because of his eccentricities, and mainly because we picked up a great deal of general information which started up new interests, and we were encouraged to think. Such teachers have their uses.

At one time or another during my stay at U.C.S. I was taught by a good many members of the staff, and I have since come to realise how much I owed at any rate to some of them. For example, there was G. J. Hawkes, a first-class schoolmaster. There was no "soft pædagogics" about his Latin lessons. We "took places", sitting on long benches or standing in form order. If you were "put on" by Hawkes you had to face up to a series of searching questions which were passed on if you could not answer them. Thus one had to know one's work thoroughly if one were to maintain one's position; and unless this could be done one quickly descended to the bottom of the class. On the other hand, a lucky answer might result in the gain of a number of places. How freely one breathed when Hawkes in his precise little voice said "Thank you. That will do."

Another fine teacher of the classics was J. W. E. Pearce, with his yellow hair and his long moustache, the ends of which he used to chew when he was annoyed. If your work were un-satisfactory he would throw the "T.B. ticket" at you with un-erring aim. He left us to run a successful preparatory school of his own. A. W. Tressler (himself an Old Gower), who in due

course coached me for an Oxford scholarship when I was in the
Sixth, afterwards went to Charterhouse. He was not only a
distinguished classic, but he had won the Taylorian scholarship in
modern languages at Oxford and was a musician of considerable
ability. "Freddy" Felkin, who also took the Classical Sixth, was
the author of the school history which was published about the
time that U.C.S. moved from Gower Street to Hampstead. Nor
must I forget F. W. Levander who taught me Greek as he had
taught my father nearly thirty years before. His versatility is
shown by the fact that he was at one time president of the
Royal Astronomical Society and was also the author of a treatise
on Greek accents. He had a sense of humour—and also a squint,
with the result that when he asked a question two boys usually
answered. His favourite maxim was "When in doubt look it
out", but we emended it to "When in doubt leave it out".

As I went up the school an increasing part of my time was
given to Latin and Greek, but I still found much to interest me
in other subjects. There were, for example, the English lessons
of John Russell—a teacher whom one can justly describe as
"inspiring". He encouraged us to think on the things that are
true, honest, lovely and of good report; and that without ever
seeming in the least didactic. At Cambridge he had come under
the influence of R. H. Quick. He was a great admirer of Pestalozzi
and had translated De Guimp's life of the great educator. He had
also written a biography of Francis Place. These facts show where
his interests lay; and he subsequently became headmaster of the
King Alfred School, Hampstead, which is a coeducational establishment run on "progressive" lines.* I was fortunate also in
learning German from two vigorous and up-to-date young
masters—W. G. Lipscombe, who was afterwards headmaster of
Bolton School, and E. R. Edwards, who became an H.M.I.
Mathematics was competently taught by George Thompson, who
was reported to be anxious to be taken for a retired army officer
when he went out by the North Western line from Euston to

* For more about John Russell and King Alfred School see W. A. C. Stewart,
*The Educational Innovators*, II, pp. 29–30.

play golf at Wembley. He used to organise periodic "problem fights", when he would introduce us to "wegular stickeller, ma boy, calc'lated to make yer sit up". I never had the advantage of going to F. W. Russell ("Baby" Russell, to distinguish him from John R.), who was senior mathematical master and afterwards went in the same capacity to Dulwich.

On any kind of science I never had a single lesson, though there was plenty of provision in the School for the teaching of this subject. It was the regular thing for members of the Science Sixth to take the London Intermediate during their course. There was also every year a strong contingent of boys who took the Preliminary Scientific (as the first medical examination was then called) before proceeding to one of the London hospitals. Chemistry used to be taught in a "theatre" at the top of the building. Here the presiding genius was Temple Orme—himself an Old Gower—who had been a master at the school since 1868 and had also taught my father. He kept a register of old boys which has formed the basis of the published lists and of the centenary volume which appeared in 1931. When eventually I became editor of the school magazine I relied much on Temple Orme's encyclopaedic knowledge of the school's history. Orme hid a heart of gold under a rather gruff exterior. He was rather proud of making himself out to be an atheist. When Tressler was outlining to me the arrangements for the opening of the new school buildings at Hampstead by King Edward VII (by that time I was at Oxford), he told me that the Archbishop of Canterbury had undertaken to perform the ceremony of dedication. He added that we ought really to invite Dr. Horton, the eminent nonconformist divine, to read a lesson from the New Testament and the Chief Rabbi one from the Old, and Temple Orme could end up by saying "Damn". Then everybody would be satisfied.

Although I never had the benefit of science lessons from Orme, my largely classical curriculum was from time to time enlivened by a lecture of more general interest which was given to the whole school. I remember one in particular delivered by Sir

William Ramsay, the father of one of my schoolfellows. Sir William was professor of chemistry in University College and he had made a reputation by the discovery of argon and other inert gases. In the particular lecture to which I refer he dealt with the liquefaction of air, which had recently been effected and which, I am told, has had important implications for the oxygen industry and the functioning of neon and similar lamps. On another occasion we had a talk by Mrs. Ormiston Chant who was also the parent of one of my contemporaries. She was well known in her day as a social reformer, and as an advocate of woman's suffrage and teetotalism. She had nursed in hospitals and organised relief work in Armenia and Crete. She also launched an attack on the Empire Music Hall where the "promenade" was a notorious resort of prostitutes. I think that she and J. L. Paton must have had a good deal in common. Mrs. Chant had travelled extensively and had lectured in various parts of the world, and her talk to us, illustrated by lantern slides, dealt with her experiences. I remember one which showed a boat-load of British bluejackets who had come to her aid when she had got into difficulties with local officials in (I think) China. This afforded us an opportunity to relax from boredom by giving a hearty cheer.

I have already shown that I was fortunate in most of the masters who taught me at U.C.S. and I am glad to be able to testify to their merits. But the staff had also its "passengers", and it is difficult to understand how some of them had obtained—or, at any rate, been confirmed in—their appointments, though in most cases they had retained them for thirty years or more. There was, for example, a wild Irishman who was always losing his temper and shouting "Confound your brutal impudence". He got the discipline he deserved. A more pathetic case was a Frenchman, under whom I made my way through Chardenal's textbook which must surely be the original source of "la plume de ma tante". His classes were a bear-garden. He had been wounded in the arm during the Franco-Prussian War and was always ready to show us the scar. He was writing an historical French grammar which, according to him, was to refute the Prussians' claim that their language was "die Muttersprache", and when published would make them "howl like wolves". We could always successfully divert his attention from the subject of the lesson by asking him how the grammar was getting on. His pronunciation of English was not always very reliable. He would tell us, for example, "If you vant to speak French vell you must be a curate" —a curious reason for taking Holy Orders. On one occasion seeing a boy idling, he cried out "Walk!" The boy in considerable perplexity stood up and began to come out towards the master's desk. This provoked a still louder "Walk, I say". At length it dawned on the culprit that this was the Gallic equivalent for the word "Work".

In spite of these weaker brethren the School, as I have said, was on the whole fortunate in the masters whom it had attracted to its service. They were for the most part good scholars and good teachers, and, what is much more important, they possessed personality and character. They were not just teaching machines, imparting or checking information like the monitors of Bell and Lancaster or their modern mechanical equivalents. They helped to influence one's attitude to life and to look beyond the subject-matter under consideration. In short they were educators and not simply teachers. There was little in those days to attract men of such calibre into the profession, and they must have entered it of deliberate choice and with a sense of vocation. Most of the staff were Cambridge men, though Hawkes, Pearce and Tressler were Oxonians. There were no grants from local authorities or elsewhere in their time to help with the heavy expenses of a university course. Yet the usual starting salary for a master in a first-grade grammar school was only about £150 a year, and in some cases as little as £120. If there was a scale—and it was by no means usual—it might rise by annual increments of £5 or £10 to a maximum of £200 or even £300.* Hardly any schools

* For details and actual examples see Appendix B and Part II, chapter iv, in Norwood and Hope, *The Higher Education of Boys in England*. The information given refers to the year 1909, and conditions were even worse at the end of the nineteenth century.

had pension schemes, though after 1902 some of the local authorities included teachers in the superannuation schemes for their officials. But for the Burnham scales teachers had to wait till 1919, and it was not until the Teachers (Superannuation) Acts of 1918, 1925 and 1956 that a pension, soon made contributory, was secured to all teachers serving in state-aided schools. Even today many independent schools have their own pension schemes.

I was brought into almost daily contact with many of the masters to whom reference has been made; but in the background was the rather shadowy figure of the Headmaster, Henry Weston Eve. At U.C.S., when I first went there, most of the boys in the lower forms had less opportunity for contact with the Head-master than is perhaps customary in most schools. The main reason for this was that we did not have—as is usual elsewhere—a daily assembly for prayers, or a chapel service, conducted by the Head. It was only for some special reason that the whole school was convened and we were able to see and hear the Headmaster. Eve was a tall and impressive figure, arrayed always in a frock-coat and a gown. His drawl and his habit of playing with his watch-chain while speaking were occasions of derisive imitation among our smaller fry. For example, we would mimic his announcement "Some vulgah little beggah—ah—has been scwibbling on the lockahs. Ah—if detected—ah—he will be dealt with most severelah." But Eve was an excellent teacher and I had the privilege of being in one of the few lower school forms that he took. It was thus that he taught me the little geography that I ever learnt at school. I remember him demonstrating the course of ocean currents by twirling a globe round and at the same time pouring ink over it.

For this reason perhaps I had more opportunities of getting to know Eve than were afforded to the average newcomer to U.C.S.; and my memories of him are pleasant ones. But it cannot be said that he was popular with the lower school. When he resigned his headship in 1898 he held an assembly to say good-bye to the School. After he had spoken, some of the VI form started to sing "For he's a jolly good fellow"; but the tune was taken up by my contemporaries, among whom I was standing, to the words

> Shut up the public houses . . .
> We don't want none of your beer.

It was not until long after I had left U.C.S. and was, as an adult, investigating its history, that I came to realise Eve's eminence as an educationist and the value of his services to the School. For this reason it may be due to his memory to attempt here some estimate of his career.

Henry Weston Eve came of yeoman stock and was born at Maldon in Essex. Educated at Mill Hill and at Rugby, he went up to Trinity College, Cambridge, of which he became a scholar in 1858. He graduated as eleventh wrangler and was elected to a fellowship. But he preferred schoolmastering to university work and was appointed to a post at Wellington College. There he remained for sixteen years, with two short intervals—one spent at Heidelberg studying chemistry under Professor Bunsen, and the other serving as an assistant commissioner to the Endowed Schools Commission. He organised the modern side at Wellington, and with his colleague De Baudiss (afterwards senior modern language master at U.C.S.) he produced the Wellington College French and German grammars. They were standard works in their day.

In 1877 Eve was appointed Headmaster of U.C.S.—my father was still a pupil there when he arrived. In those days the School was understaffed and the staff were underpaid. But Eve, while he was at Cambridge, had inherited a moderate fortune; and on becoming a headmaster he devoted the greater part of his professional income to supplementing the emoluments of his colleagues. To quote his obituary notice in *The Times*: "Most generous and hospitable of men, he spared neither purse nor person in promoting the interests of the school." There is no doubt that during his twenty-three years' headmastership Eve did an enormous amount to strengthen the School's position and to develop its activities both in the class-room and outside it. In

particular he had given the utmost encouragement to the School
games. When he first came to U.C.S. there was only one School
eleven which played on casual pitches at Lords or on the Eton
and Middlesex ground which is now covered by houses. But it
was owing to Eve's initiative and beneficence that accommodation for games was made available at Willesden Green; and when
the School ground at Neasden was purchased it was appropriately
named the Eve Field in honour of him. When the School gymnasium was being built by private subscription Eve again contributed lavishly.

Coming as he did from a boarding school to what was pre-
dominantly a day school (though some of the masters had
boarding houses), Eve tried to import into our organisation some
of the features of a more closely knit community. It was owing to
him that the system of consulting masters, already described, was
introduced. He also (unlike some eminent headmasters) seems to
have been *persona grata* with his colleagues. One of them, writing
of him, says: "His sympathy with all engaged in the calling (i.e.
of a schoolmaster), and his sagacity in dealing with them were
equally untiring and keen." But his educational activities were not
confined to the School. He served on the committee of the
Headmasters' Conference, for many years he acted as Dean of the
College of Preceptors, and he was a council member of both the
Girls' Public Day School Trust and of the Teachers' Guild. In
appearance, as I have said, he was dignified, tall and broad-
shouldered. He had excellent health and unusual muscular
strength. In his time he had been a vigorous rider and runner.
Even to the end of his days he used to run up the staircase of the
Athenæum (of which he was an habitué) two steps at a time. He
was also noted for his sociability and hospitality. He lived at a
house in Gordon Square, where he was looked after by his two
sisters until his marriage with Florence Gross, who was a sister-
in-law of George Eliot.

Such then was the man who became Headmaster of U.C.S.
in my father's last year there, and who retired at the end of my
first year. Perhaps neither of us had either time or opportunity to

J. L. Paton (see Chapter 11).

"Vewel Jearn" (see page 119).

Queen Victoria at Temple Bar, on her way to St. Paul's for the
Diamond Jubilee thanksgiving, June 22nd, 1897 (see page 126).

realise Eve's true worth; but I am glad to have been able since to form a more just estimate of him. *The Times* obituary notice, which I have already quoted, described him as "generous and helpful in every relation of life", and said "The charm of his gracious memory will endure".

## CHAPTER 11

# John Lewis Paton

EVE was succeeded by a man of completely different type—
John Lewis Paton. Great as Eve was, Paton was something
greater. I regard him as among the most outstanding headmasters
of his time and as one of the finest men that I have ever been
privileged to know. I was for five years a boy under him at
U.C.S., and during the latter part of that time was in his Sixth
form and in daily contact with him. I was also in close touch with
him during my seven and a half university years. I served under
him for a short time at Manchester and during that period I
lived in his house. Afterwards we corresponded regularly and met
from time to time; and when finally he retired and came to live
in Kent he was a fairly close neighbour of mine. All this means
that the impressions of Paton that I formed as a school-boy are
inevitably much mixed up and overlaid with memories of him
during the subsequent stages of our friendship. Hitherto in this
book I have tried to recapture, to some extent at any rate, my
contemporary point of view and interests when describing the
various stages in my education. The only conspicuous exception
is the account of H. W. Eve given at the end of the last chapter.
But I am bound to build up my portrait of Paton from what I
knew of him all along. It has always been a matter of real regret
to me that no full-scale biography of him has been attempted.
Far less eminent persons have been fully documented.

John Lewis Alexander Paton—or "J. L. P.", as he was generally
called—was proud of his descent from Scottish covenanting
ancestors, and his father, John Brown Paton, had been principal

of the Congregational Theological College at Nottingham. He was at school at Halle, in Germany, before being sent to Shrewsbury where he eventually became head boy. There he benefited by the high standard of classical teaching which had been established by Benjamin Hall Kennedy, who had been headmaster of Shrewsbury from 1836 to 1866; Paton entered the school eight years after his retirement. But J. L. P. was no narrow classic. He used to relate how his interest in English Literature had been kindled by hearing his schoolfellow, Owen Seaman (who afterwards became editor of *Punch*), recite Tennyson's *Idylls of the King* in the dormitory at night. In 1882 Paton was elected a scholar of St. John's College, Cambridge, and in due course became Senior Classic in Part I of the Tripos and obtained a first class in Part II, with special distinctions in language and history. He was also second Chancellor's medallist. He gained a fellowship at St. John's; but after a year's teaching at the Leys' School he was invited by Dr. Percival (afterwards Bishop of Hereford) to take the Sixth form lower bench at Rugby, and to act as tutor to the town boys.

Throughout his career at Cambridge and at Rugby Paton had retained his staunch adherence to nonconformity and a keen interest in social work, especially among boys. He could be seen parading the streets of Rugby in charge of a troop of the Boys' Brigade, and on Sundays he would go off on his bicycle to take the service and preach at a local dissenting conventicle. All this may have caused some lifting of the eyebrows in certain circles, but it did not prevent Paton from staying ten years at Rugby.

Such then was our new headmaster, for Paton, at the age of 35, was appointed to U.C.S. in 1898. In contrast to the tall, dignified, imposing, bewhiskered Eve, J. L. P. was barely of middle height, sturdy of build, clean-shaven, strong-mouthed, with the fresh-complexioned, weather-beaten appearance of a sailor. His brilliant blue eyes seemed to look either right through you or else away to some far-distant horizon. Like Eve he had excellent health and was never off duty; but he suffered occasionally from devastating headaches—the result, I suspect, of overwork.

He cared not a whit for conventions, and, having no wife to look after him, lacked the corrective from which married men benefit. On a day when there was to be a meeting of the school governors, or of the Board of Education Consultative Committee of which he was a member, he would cycle down to school from his house in Hampstead wearing a morning coat and a pair of "plus-fours" (he never sported a hat), while his more orthodox trousers were obviously in the brown paper parcel which was tied on behind. I well remember, also, how on an important evening occasion at school Paton appeared with a large piece of bright red brace showing at one side of his dress shirt-front.

In some of his views J. L. P. retained the rather puritanical rigidity of the nonconformist tradition which he had inherited. He was a convinced total-abstainer and non-smoker. He was fiercely opposed to any form of betting or gambling. The positive side of his inhibitions expressed itself in his earnest advocacy of the open-air, cold-bath régime to which I have already referred when speaking of the "Answers to Correspondents" in the *Boy's Own Paper*. When, as a senior boy, one was invited by Paton to dine at his house, he would take his guests for a preliminary cross-country run over Hampstead Heath, himself setting the pace. He encouraged boys to learn to swim and organised life-saving classes. He was, in fact, all his life long something of a Boy Scout, and he gave whole-hearted support to the movement when it was inaugurated by Baden Powell in 1908. Even before that he was running school camps. I remember one at Walberswick, in Suffolk. It was conducted on much the same lines as those afterwards adopted by the Scouts, except that our cooking was done by the school beadle, William. We had treks in the surrounding country and sing-songs in the evening; and Paton himself led the morning bathing parade, even when the wind was at its nippiest. When, after leaving us, J. L. P. became High Master of Manchester Grammar School, he extended these open-air holiday activities. Under his inspiration walking-parties of boys were taken to France and over the Alps to Italy, to the Black Forest and to Norway. He was always anxious to promote friendly international relations by means of such excursions and by foreign exchanges. Today these efforts are commonplaces of school-life; but they were almost unknown at the beginning of the present century, and Paton may be regarded as a pioneer in this respect. Nor must I forget how he inculcated the dignity (and usefulness) of manual labour. At U.C.S. he organised squads who had the job of painting the iron supports of the fence round the School playing-field—himself wielding the brush with the best of us. At Manchester, while I was there, it became necessary to level part of the cricket ground, and we all turned to with spades and wheelbarrows, Paton again setting us the example. During the 1914–18 war, also, he kept his boys busy at harvesting and other agricultural work. He was, in short, a complete exponent of the doctrine of "mens sana in corpore sano". He took as much interest in the physical welfare of his charges as in their intellectual and spiritual welfare, because he believed that these things act and react one upon the other.

J. L. P. was a most inspiring teacher—alive, humorous, stimulating, thorough. He had an intense interest in the individual boy and the gift—so useful to a headmaster—of knowing something about every member of the School. This was true even at Manchester where he had over a thousand pupils. His interest was equally keen whether you were in the Sixth or at the bottom of the school. This was evidenced by the insight shown in his "headmaster's remarks" on our monthly reports—a system which was unknown in the days of Eve, but which was introduced by Paton. More than this, if you had an illness which necessitated a prolonged absence from school, he would write to you or even come and see you. When I was about 17 I had a very severe attack of measles. I have preserved several letters, written in German, which he sent to me at this time.

Paton was, of course, primarily a classic and I remember chiefly his lessons in Latin and Greek. But I have already alluded to his interest in English Literature. At Rugby he used to invite the boys to his house on Sunday evenings in order to read English plays, and at Manchester he allowed the school Literary

Society to hold its meetings in his private room. When I was at
U.C.S. I was privileged for three years to be in a weekly essay
class in which all the members of the various VI's were collected;
and I still possess some of the compositions which I wrote during
this period. The subjects are mainly literary, and J. L. P.'s love
for Tennyson is reflected in our comments on *Ulysses*, *The Lotus
Eaters* and *The Palace of Art*. But sometimes a theme was taken
from social history—e.g. "The Influence of Geography upon
History", "Primitive Civilisations", or "The Brick, the Plough
and the Ship". Occasionally our aesthetic judgements would be
brought into play, as for example in "The Feeling for Natural
Scenery" or "Art and Life" (this latter was after a talk about
Ruskin and William Morris). J. L. P. was a great admirer of
German literature and his school days at Halle had implanted in
him a permanent interest in the old romantic Germany which is
now as remote as the romantic movement in this country. For
France and French culture he had little sympathy—and in fact he
knew little about either. I suspect that he identified them with
the "Gay Paree" associations, or with the free-thought of the
"philosophers" and their successors, which shocked orthodox
nineteenth-century nonconformity.

Although not musical himself, J. L. P. did his utmost—short
of including music in the curriculum—to encourage a love of it.
He also believed that art, and especially handicraft, should form
part of every boy's education; and although he was not able—
largely owing to problems of accommodation and staff—to give
much expression to this belief at U.C.S., he had a more free hand
at Manchester and made the most of the opportunity. But he gave
every support to the various "out-of-class activities" in which we
engaged. He even organised an exhibition of hobbies; and when
asked whether it might include a collection of caricatures of the
masters he replied "Yes, if you begin with me". The first prize
for a drawing of J. L. P. himself was won by the son of A. S.
Boyd, a well-known contributor to *Punch*. This inspired Owen
Seaman to compose a poem which appeared in the August 6th,
1902 issue of this periodical. It is entitled *A Punch Staff-College*,

and it contrasts the attitude in this respect of "Salopia", when they were both pupils there, with that which apparently obtained at U.C.S. under Paton. It ends with the verse:

> Macte! and ever may the round
> Of graver duties leave you free
> So to support a training-ground
> Of younger Tenniels to be.

In 1903 Paton left U.C.S. to become High Master of Manchester Grammar School. He quickly made his personality felt not only in the life of the School itself, but in that of the great city also. As I have already said, I had the very great privilege of living for a time in his house in Broughton Park. I thus got to know him well and to realise something of his greatness. He led the most simple of lives. His bedroom, which was also his library, contained practically no furniture except a small, iron truckle-bed; though in the summer he usually slept out under a "bivvy" tent in the garden. He had practically no sense of taste— a fact of which his aged housekeeper used to take advantage, though this sometimes made things trying for other members of the household. His acts of mercy and charity were manifold— though most of them were known only to the recipients, for he always did good by stealth. His house in Broughton Park was always full of "lame dogs"—boys whose parents had had to move away and could no longer afford to keep their sons at M.G.S., old boys who were finding it difficult to maintain themselves during university vacations, impecunious young foreigners who had come over to study in this country. All alike were guests— welcome without any question of payment. Nor were his beneficent activities confined to members of the School or to students. He was a frequent visitor to Strangeways Prison and was particularly interested in the reclamation of young criminals. A man who cared not twopence for dignity or convention was bound to be criticised in some quarters. He certainly was in Manchester; and I have no doubt that there were parents—and possibly masters and governors, too—at U.C.S. who contrasted him unfavourably with the dignified and academic Eve. There were also some people who tended to be put off by his rather uncompromising nonconformity. But even his critics recognised and respected his sincerity and his high ideals of service. In the rest of us he inspired an enthusiastic devotion.

When he retired from Manchester in 1924 Paton, after a preliminary lecturing tour for the National Council of Education in Canada, was appointed president of the Government Memorial College at St. John's, Newfoundland (it is now the Memorial University). In the course of his tenure of this post he not only carried out the administrative duties for which he was responsible, but he also took a large share in the teaching. I remember him saying in a letter to me (I was at the time headmaster of a grammar school) how he envied us the ease with which we at home could obtain well-qualified and efficient members for our staffs—a condition which certainly does not obtain today. Under Paton the status of the Memorial College rose and it became possible for students to take the first two years of a degree course there before moving on to one of the universities in Canada.

In 1933 Paton returned to this country and settled down, with his sister Mary, in a house on the Pilgrims' Way at Kemsing, in Kent. He died in 1946. At his memorial service held in St. Dunstan's Church, Fleet Street, it was very evident—and also very understandable—that Manchester should claim him as their own. But I like to remember that he first belonged to us.

I have always felt that Paton was more at home in Manchester than at U.C.S. He once said to me, just before leaving us, "I am looking forward to being able to do something for poor boys". The conditions at U.C.S., indeed, were against him. The population of the Bloomsbury squares had moved out to the suburbs, and most of our boys now came in by train from various parts of North London. The religious toleration and breadth of curriculum which had marked out the School in earlier days were now the common property of many other London schools. For some years, even in the days of Eve, the numbers in the School had been decreasing. Paton made an attempt to arrest this decline by taking in a group of scholars, financed by the London County

Council, who formed a Commercial Side. The experiment was not a success. These boys were already well above the ordinary age for entrance, and they formed a self-conscious clique with a curriculum all their own. They were never really assimilated into the School, and the "Commercials" were always looked down upon by the rest of us. After a few years the scheme was abandoned; and although at a later period the school did for a time take a small proportion of L.C.C. "free-placers", it soon re-assumed its independent status. But it was obvious that the only chance for its continued success would be complete removal to an area from which most of its pupils were now drawn. But all this must have involved many difficulties for Paton. As he said in a letter to me after he had got to Manchester, and I had gone up to Oxford, "We came through hard days, and came through without ever losing hope". So it was under his régime that the plans for moving school were adumbrated. The preparatory de-partment, taking boys aged 7 to 13, had been opened at Holly Hill, Hampstead, as far back as 1891, and at the initiative of H. W. Eve. It was at last decided to move the Upper School to the same neighbourhood. The work, begun by Paton, was carried through by his successor, Dr. H. J. Spenser. A magnificent new school was erected on a site at Frognal, Hampstead, and this was opened on July 26th, 1907 by King Edward VII. The build-ings—as has been said—were dedicated by the Archbishop of Canterbury. Since then the School has flourished in its new home. May it long continue to do so!

CHAPTER 12

# Activities, in and out of School

LIKE other schools, we had a large number of "out-of-class activities", and many of them owed a great deal to Eve's encouragement. The Scientific Society and the Swimming Club dated from the 1870's, as did also the School Library and the Reading Room. There were flourishing Chess and Photographic Clubs; but my chief interest was in the Debating Society which had been founded as far back as 1857. Here I was an assiduous attendant. It was a great opportunity to show off one's powers as an orator and a humorist. On one occasion, when we were discussing the pros and cons of cremation, an Irish member began his speech by saying "Gentlemen, this is a grave and burning question". At another time the proposer of a motion in favour of total abstinence had the effectiveness of his opening speech seriously marred by the fact that someone had placed an empty bottle of Bass under his chair, where it was invisible to the speaker but could be plainly seen by the audience. No form of music had any place in the school curriculum, but there were periodic attempts to form a brass band which used to practise in the room adjoining that in which the debates were held; and when the two functions coincided raids and reprisals sometimes resulted. We were, however, given opportunities for community singing out of class-room hours, and we had our own *U.C.S. Song Book*. Substantially it was an edition of John Farmer's *Gaudeamus*; but it contained also a number of German songs—German was always a strong subject in the school—as well as

some special items all our own. These included amongst others
the school song "Where our founders led", and some macaronic
verses which concluded:

> May Fortuna, semper fausta,
> All your steadfast labours bless;
> Floreas et in æternum,
> Alma Mater, U.C.S.

The School Cadet Corps, as far as my experience went, tended
to be rather looked down upon by the members of the Upper
School; but it had been in existence since the middle of the nineteenth century. It formed a company of the London Rifle Brigade
and in the 1880's was the largest Cadet Corps in London. It usually
formed a guard of honour at the Lord Mayor's banquet; but it
justified its existence in a more serious manner at the time of the
South African War. Although the School certainly had no
military traditions, over 100 old boys volunteered for service, and
twelve of them lost their lives. A bronze tablet was put up to
their memory, and this was unveiled by Joseph Chamberlain
(complete with eye-glass and orchid), then Colonial Secretary
and himself an old boy of the School. Another activity of a very
different type was the U.C.S. Club for Working Boys, which was
started in Clerkenwell and afterwards transferred to Bermondsey.
It corresponded to the missions which some other schools have
instituted. It had been initiated by Eve in 1886, for many years it
was organised by one of his colleagues, J. S. Masterman, with the
assistance of a number of old boys and senior members of the
School. We all contributed to its support.

Travelling and homework together accounted for a good deal
of my time that was not spent in school; but, for all that, I
managed to keep up my outside interests. One of the chief of
these was music. After I had entered U.C.S. I still continued to
have piano lessons and to practise. But my main delight was to
explore my father's quite considerable library of piano works. I
was a fair reader (though I have never been able to remember
music), and I was not discouraged whatever the result was like,

though at times—as I have already suggested—it must have been exceedingly trying for the other members of the household. It was in this way that I became familiar with most of Beethoven's sonatas, some of the compositions of Schumann and Chopin, Schubert's *Impromptus*, *Moments Musicaux* and piano sonatas, Grieg's *Lyric Pieces*, of which we had a bound volume, and the contents of various "Albums" devoted to the works of lesser, though still distinguished, nineteenth-century composers. I also kept up my interest in oratorio by playing (or trying to play) the piano score of Handel's chief works, Mendelssohn's *Elijah*, *St. Paul* and *Hymn of Praise*, or Spohr's *Last Judgment* (Spohr was a popular composer in those days). It was not until I got to Oxford that I discovered the choral sublimities of J. S. Bach—the *B mi. Mass*, the *Passions*, the *Magnificat*, the *Christmas Oratorio* and the Church Cantatas. Interest in oratorio was fostered not only by periodic visits to the Handel Festival (and on New Year's Day to the Albert Hall to hear *Messiah*), but also by performances given by local societies. All over the London suburbs in those days there were groups of enthusiastic amateurs who from time to time would put on a Handel oratorio, varied occasionally perhaps by *Elijah* or some lesser work like Gaul's *Holy City* or Sullivan's *Golden Legend* or Barnetts' *Ancient Mariner*. These societies had as a rule to engage professional soloists and some, at any rate, of the players in the orchestra; but the sale of tickets usually covered expenses. Small amateur choral societies of this type work under heavy handicaps nowadays owing to the greatly increased cost of the adjuncts from outside—and possibly also owing to the competition of broadcast concerts. But for a schoolboy who was keenly interested in music they provided in that bygone age a wonderful opportunity of becoming familiar with the choral works particularly of Handel, who held a place in popular esteem which has since perhaps been taken by J. S. Bach.

When I approached my sixteenth birthday my father offered, as a present, to pay for twelve lessons on either the 'cello or the organ. It was a difficult decision to make, but finally I came down in favour of the organ. If I had chosen the 'cello I might have had the fun of being able to play in an orchestra. I tried many years later to rectify this omission by learning the double-bass; but pressure of work made proper practice impossible and eventually I had to give this up. In my choice of the organ I suppose I was influenced by the example of my father who—as I have said—was himself a performer on this instrument. As a matter of fact I had already been experimenting with the organ and that also influenced my decision. So I became a pupil of Dr. Walker Robson who was a brilliant executant and a first-rate teacher. I used to have lessons with him either at his church or else at the London Organ School in Princes Street, near Oxford Circus. It possessed a curious instrument on the Casson system*—a kind of forerunner of the modern "extension" organ. Dr. Walker Robson gave me a good grounding in organ technique and awakened in me an enthusiasm which has grown with age and experience. I started—as all organ students seem to do—with the eight short Preludes and Fugues of Bach; but I continued to have lessons and it was not long before I was tackling more tricky pieces, and eventually I graduated to some of the "classics"—the St. Anne, the F minor, the D major, and even the Wedge. I also learnt pieces by César Franck, Guilmant, Widor, Dubois and Gigout— I have always rather liked the late nineteenth-century French school of organ composers who now seem to be much neglected —and in addition to these a couple of Mendelssohn's Organ Sonatas, some Rheinberger, the Schumann Canons and Studies, a Handel Concerto (No. 4), and a good many other things. For a young organist it was a flying start and it also opened the way for me to an entirely new musical field. Although by this time I was working for a classical scholarship, and therefore did not get much opportunity for practice, I never lost touch with either the piano or organ.

There was another interest to which I devoted a good deal of my leisure throughout the time that I was at U.C.S. This was a family magazine called The Omnibus. It had been started in 1897 by two cousins and myself and it ran successfully for six years.

* It is described in J. W. Hinton, Organ Construction, pp. 184–6 and plate xvii.

We used to issue four numbers annually and they were sent round by post according to a rota. We interested some of our friends in the venture, and even one or two of our elders; and this led to the formation of "The Omnibus Magazine Club", which used to have an annual "social"—a party for the members, kindly provided by the parents of one or other of us. The contributions were extremely varied and in some cases reached quite a high standard. In particular we had a number of gifted artists who sent us frontispieces and other illustrations, as well as illuminated covers. A series of these one year was provided by my artist uncle from Wedgwoods'. He made the centre of interest in each drawing a female figure representing the appropriate season. The lady who typified "Spring" occasioned some disapproving comment among our more nonconformist Victorian elders because, like the Rhine-maiden in Hans Breitmann's *Ballad*, she "hadn't got nodings on".

Sometimes my father would contribute an article—that being in his line of business. One of my cousins (who afterwards became a clergyman) used to write upon serious topics and composed nature-poems in the Wordsworthian vein. The other cousin, who had a pretty wit, wrote parodies and humorous verse; he was also the author of a school story. But the bulk of the work fell on me because I was the editor. I soon learnt the journalistic trick of "mugging things up". I contributed informative articles on varied topics ranging from "The History of Ecclesiastical Vestments" and "Appendicitis" (King Edward VII's coronation had just been postponed because he had contracted this disease) to "The Biblical Conception of Hell" and "Evils wrought by Fashion". Or else I tried to emulate my younger cousin by writing light verse. But my *magna opera* were some serial stories which purported to have been written by "Vewel Jearn"—and were, of course, a very long way behind the great original. There was, for example, *The Green Circle*—the exploits of a piratical airship (operated by helicopters), which finally made an air-raid on London; *To Another World*, which anticipated space travel because it described a visit to Mars; and

*Destruction*, in which an abortive attempt to make a tunnel through the earth to Australia, by means of a disintegrating ray, results in the ocean rushing into the hole so formed. This causes an explosion in the interior of the earth which blows the satellite to bits so that it falls into the sun. I wonder if that—like so many of the stories of Jules Verne himself—is destined to be prophetic. We worked the "Vewel Jearn" idea in several ways. We had, for example, an interview with him, illustrated by a photograph in which I wore dark glasses and a false beard and moustache. At the time of the Boer War, when public opinion on the Continent was largely anti-British, "Vewel Jearn" would write indignant letters to the editor (in execrable French), which were of course duly published in *The Omnibus*. It was all great fun and I think there was none of us who did not feel regret when the three chief contributors went up to the university and *The Omnibus* ceased to run.

Music and my editorial duties did not leave me a great deal of time for out-of-school reading. However, I continued to enjoy the *Boy's Own Paper* and a similar (though not quite so improving) periodical called *The Captain*. I was also a regular reader of the *Railway Magazine* which was started about 1897. But I did not get much pleasure out of the works of the classical novelists and poetry of almost any kind did not appeal to me at all. It is curious that, although at school and afterwards at Oxford I ploughed my way through reams of Latin and Greek verse, yet I have as a rule found it difficult to appreciate poetry and rarely read it for its own sake. All the same, I did manage to do some serious reading out of school. In the Sixth form I had been introduced to Carlyle's *Heroes* and *Sartor Resartus*. This made me interested in the Sage of Chelsea in spite of (perhaps, because of) his choppy style; and I went on to read not only *Past and Present*, but even the whole of the *French Revolution*. I also read some Ruskin, and for light relief I had recourse to the delightful "Breakfast Table" books. But what I liked chiefly to do was to poke about in my father's library and read extracts rather than whole volumes. I gave considerable attention to what Lamb called βιβλία ἀββλία—gazetteers, encyclopædias, *Whitaker's Almanac* and reference books of that type. It all bore fruit when at the beginning of each term the whole school had to take a General Knowledge examination. As Paton once wrote in his "Head-master's Remarks" on my monthly report, "Omne tulit punctum qui miscuit utile dulci".

Although I had got the habit of reading widely and was encouraged to explore both at school and at home, I was less interested in newspapers. The change in the character of current journalism is one of the most striking features of the period with which I am dealing. Sir Richard Ensor* speaks of the "extremely dignified type of journalism conducted with a high sense of personal responsibility" which was characteristic of the 1880's. Of this category *The Times* and the *Daily Telegraph* still exist, and there are several provincial newspapers of similar calibre; but the *Morning Post, Standard, Daily News, Daily Chronicle* and several others have all disappeared. In their place we have seen the rise of "another type, far less responsible and far less in-tellectual, but far more widely sold". The pioneer of this decline was Alfred Harmsworth, whose contribution to national cultural and educational standards was signalised by his elevation to the peerage as Lord Northcliffe. The exploitation of sensationalism and the presentation of "stories" rather than of straight news dates from about the 1890's, while I was still at school; but I do not think I was affected by it. Besides the "gutter press", as it was termed by the people who did not like it, there were "low-brow" productions of a chatty or supposedly humorous type, such as *Tit-bits* and *Answers, Comic Cuts* and *Ally Sloper's Half Holiday*, but it never occurred to me to patronise them. They were the sort of literature that "board school boys" read and it would have been *infra dig* to have anything to do with them. If I had brought a copy into the house, I am sure it would have been promptly confiscated. A more reputable type of litera-ture was provided by magazines such as the *Strand* in which the Sherlock Holmes stories first appeared. *Blackwood's Magazine*

* *Oxford History of England, 1870–1914,* p. 310.

(founded in 1817) and *Chambers' Journal* (dating from 1832) were still appearing and were perhaps of a more definitely literary type. There were also several evening papers of the "dignified and responsible" type. I remember in particular the *Globe*, the *Pall Mall Gazette*, and the *Westminster Gazette*. The weekly cartoon in the last-named, drawn by Carruthers Gould—the father of one of my schoolfellows—was a very popular feature.

Another feature of these evening papers was the double acrostic which was published every Saturday. My father and a few friends, who included two doctors, a business man and a member of a publishing firm, formed a small acrostic-solving group who used to meet every week at each others' houses. Over a cup of coffee the week's acrostics in the three papers were discussed and the final solution was drawn up and sent in. On quite a few occasions the group were successful in winning a prize. In my later 'teens I was privileged to take part in these acrostic-solving discussions, and I even decided to have a double acrostic competition in the *Omnibus* of which I was at the time the editor. I can remember only one of the lights—

> This indicates there's inflammation
> And often it is—information!

I hope it was not all so easy as this.

It was during my last summer holidays at school that I went abroad for the first time. The party consisted of my father and stepmother, and two of my cousins—a boy and a girl of approximately my own age—as well as myself. We crossed from Folkestone to Boulogne and then rumbled all through the night across northern France, arriving at Basel in time for breakfast. Thence we went on to Lucerne where we stayed for a few days. We explored the town and its environs. We saw the "Dance of Death" on the covered bridge and we heard an organ recital, including the inevitable "storm", in the cathedral. Thence we moved on to a village called Weggis at the foot of the Rigi. I believe that it afterwards became notorious as the headquarters of an international betting organisation, and that it is now a large and fashionable resort. But in those days it can have had only a few hundred inhabitants together with three or four small hotels. My people were accommodated in one of the latter, but I had a bedroom at a "dépendance"—the house where the parish priest lived. The ground floor was devoted to store-rooms and a strong smell of onions and paraffin used to pervade the whole establishment. The priest's quarters were on the first floor, and he was looked after by an aged housekeeper. My room was an attic containing one of those huge German stoves, covered with tiles, which are no doubt very comforting during the continental winter. I used to try out my German on the priest who was a friendly soul and had a sense of humour. When I was at a loss for a word I would supply the Latin equivalent—a practice which caused him great delight. On Sundays after Mass he would come in, still wearing all his vestments except his chasuble, and play cards and drink black coffee with the sacristan.

We spent at least a month at Weggis. On several occasions we walked up the Rigi, and we ascended Pilatus and the Bürgenstock by means of the funicular railway. We went for drives along the Axenstrasse; we made expeditions to the Tellskapelle and Küssnacht, so that I was able to see the actual setting of Schiller's *Wilhelm Tell*, which not long before I had been reading in class. On one occasion when walking with my father we went into a small inn in search of refreshment. The host greeted us in quite passable English and then said "I have English vine. Would you like English vine?" We asked him to let us have a look at it, whereupon he produced two bottles marked 'PALE ALE' and cried triumphantly "See, English vine—pahlay ahlay!"

The whole holiday, in short, for a schoolboy was an educative experience of the greatest value because it brought so much that was both new and interesting and that could never have been supplied by holidays in this country. There was, for example, the fascination of hearing a foreign language spoken wherever one went—and that language German, which was my favourite at school. There was the novelty of the meals—coffee, rolls and honey for breakfast and a four-course dinner in the evening; and in between one could eat green figs at ten centimes apiece. I also got a good deal of fun out of making a collection in a notebook (which I have preserved) of the day to day notices which were displayed in public—e.g. FRISCH GESTRICHEN, EINGANG VERBOTEN, LADEN ZU VERMIETEN, ZUM SCHUTZE DES PUBLIKUMS GEWIDMET. This holiday again provided the first opportunities that I had had of attending Roman Catholic churches and of witnessing the dramatic splendours of the Latin Mass.

This trip to Switzerland formed a kind of bridge between my leaving school and my going up to Oxford. It was the first of many visits to various parts of the Continent. In those days travel and accommodation were cheap and there was normally no need for a passport. One could move about almost, if not quite, as freely as in one's own country, and there was no restriction on the amount of money one could take or bring back. I am thankful to have been able to make the most of conditions like that while they lasted.

CHAPTER 13

# The Apogee of Imperialism

THE period of my childhood and youth—that is to say, the last phase of Queen Victoria's reign—was remarkable for a great upsurge of imperialistic sentiment. Hitherto the solidarity of the Empire, as an ideal to be aimed at, had not been widely held; but now the individualist self-sufficiency of an earlier age gave place to something more vivid and emotional. Catch-phrases like "the white man's burden", "Greater Britain", "The Empire upon which the sun never sets" became popular; and if you did not much care for this sort of thing you were branded as a "Little Englander". The movement was due in some part to the rise of new rivals—Germany and the United States—whose efficiency and natural resources obviously transcended our own. Greater interest in, and greater co-operation with, the "Colonies"—as (with the exception of India) they were always called—might help us to redress the balance. These aspirations were fostered by exponents of several different types. Statesmen like Joseph Chamberlain, historians like Froude and Seeley, poets like Rudyard Kipling and Henry Newbolt, and pioneers in the field like Cecil Rhodes, all contributed. The *Daily Mail*, which had been founded in 1896 by Alfred Harmsworth and which gave a new slant to English journalism, spared no pains to fan the flame of popular Jingoism. The movement expressed itself in other ways too. In 1884 the first of several Colonial Conferences was held and an Imperial Federation League was formed. In 1893 an extensive and imposing Imperial Institute was erected at South Kensington, though in the event it proved something of a white elephant. Two of the most popular exhibitions organised during the 1890's at Earl's Court by Mr. Imre Kiralfy (who apparently was not a British subject) dealt one with India and the other with the "Colonies". A B.B.C. broadcaster has even pointed out that in 1884 The Empire Theatre was opened in Leicester Square. "Its name was a new one calculated to appeal to a new generation."* Towards the end of the period Canada issued a postage-stamp showing the British Empire (naturally on the Mercator projection) in red, and bearing the inscription "We hold a vaster Empire than has been". It was as if one were to put a notice on one's front-gate to say "I have a larger income than anyone else in this road". This, then, was the attitude which increased in popularity during the last two decades of the Victorian era; but it did not go unchallenged. Gladstone had striven consistently against the flowing tide, but by this time his political influence was waning. None the less, as my family tradition remained constant to Gladstonism, we were more likely to err on the side of the "Little Englander" than of the "Jingo". But for a boy in his early 'teens the problems involved were of little concern, and one was easily affected by the spirit of the age.

The most intense expression of *fin-de-siècle* imperialism was furnished by the celebration of Queen Victoria's Diamond Jubilee in 1897. With two of my cousins I was taken by an uncle to see the procession which marked this event. We were privileged to have seats on the north side of Trafalgar Square in a stand which had been reserved for members of the London County Council and their families. We had not only a splendid view, but also the advantage of recourse, while waiting for the show, to a well-stocked refreshment bar at the back of the stand. The procession itself was a glorification of imperialism, and it owed a good deal to the inspiration of the Colonial Secretary, our distinguished Old Gower Joseph Chamberlain. It was of course—like all such processions—primarily a display of the armed forces; but they were collected from every corner of the British Empire. In addition to representative regiments from the United

* *Ideas and Beliefs of the Victorians.*, p. 326.

Kingdom there were slouch-hatted Mounted Rifles from Australia, from Canada and from South Africa. There were black-faced Hausas from Nigeria and negroes of the West India Regiment. There were even Chinamen from Hong-Kong and Dyaks from the State of North Borneo. But the most brilliant spectacle of the whole show was provided by the turbaned contingents sent by the native princes of India, with their bright green or red and gold uniforms and their flashing accoutrements. At frequent intervals there were military bands—so frequent that it was often possible to hear two of them at once, producing a curious medley of sounds. I was greatly impressed by the cavalry drummers with their two timpani slung one on each side of the horse's neck; and I watched with admiration their dexterity in crossing the drumsticks, first on this side and then on that. Perhaps one of these "timps" was the very drum that I had seen in course of construction at the ancestral "works".

After the military cavalcade came the representatives of foreign powers. Conspicuous among them was the German Emperor, William II, in a gorgeous uniform of white and gold, and with a shining helmet on the top of which was a golden eagle with outspread wings. I wonder whether, like Blucher, he was thinking to himself "Was für Beute!" It might have seemed an anticlimax when, after all this pomp and military display, came an open carriage in which sat an old lady of 78, clad in widow's weeds; but I am sure that there were few among the vast crowds which witnessed the procession who felt that this was so. Queen Victoria, although for long she had taken little part in public life, to those of us who lived during the closing years of her life was already a legend—a kind of fabulous person who gathered up all the imperialist traditions which characterised the last two decades of her reign, and which most people by this time were taking for granted. The Diamond Jubilee marked the apogee of that age.

Three and a half years later I witnessed another procession— this time in Oxford Terrace, a turning out of the Edgware Road. On January 22nd, 1901 Queen Victoria had died at Osborne in the Isle of Wight. The coffin was brought to London and carried through streets hung with purple and black to Paddington station whence it was taken to Windsor. There was another great military display, with bands playing Chopin's Funeral March, or the slow movement *sulla morte d'un' Eroe* from Beethoven's A♭ piano sonata, or—most impressive of all—Handel's Dead March in *Saul*. It was difficult to realise what had happened. Queen Victoria had seemed a stable and permanent element in the world in which we lived. One could hardly imagine a different régime. It is extraordinary how a widow who had lived so long in retirement could have counted for so much in the life of ordinary folk such as those among whom I lived, especially perhaps as my family were inclined towards "progressive" ideas and were not normally much impressed by royalties. Yet so it was; and with the passing of Queen Victoria even a schoolboy realised that the end of an era had been reached.

Another change of sentiment which marked the latter years of Queen Victoria's reign was shown by a new attitude on the part of the middle classes towards the armed forces. As G. M. Trevelyan has pointed out, "Service in the army was regarded by the middle and working classes as disgraceful—except in time of war".* My family fully shared this view. They would have endorsed Wellington's dictum that "our army is composed of the scum of the earth"†—though I doubt if they had any first-hand evidence on the matter. My father used to quote the anecdote about the army officer who was so stupid that even the other officers noticed it; and the brainless or dissolute young man of fashion who held a commission was a frequent target for witticisms and criticisms in *Punch*. But, as Kipling has pointed out,

> It's Tommy this an' Tommy that, an' 'Chuck him out, the brute.'
> But it's 'Saviour of 'is country' when the guns begin to shoot.

The navy was regarded differently. It had always been our sure shield against the envy of less happier lands. But however much

* *English Social History*, p. 584.
† P. H. Stanhope (Lord Mahon), *Notes of Conversations with the Duke of Wellington*, p. 14.

one might dislike what the armed forces stand for, it seemed perhaps unreasonable to despise the army—and the army alone—on moral, or any other, grounds. So long as men prefer to settle their disputes by murdering each other on an ever-increasing scale and by ever more elaborate and expensive means, it is surely illogical to criticise those who have the unpleasant, and often extremely hazardous, duty of carrying out those measures. It is like ostracising the hangman in a community where capital punishment is still a legal penalty. However, with the spread of the imperialist sentiment there went also a glamorising of the army, as well as of the navy; and this spread to the middle-classes, whatever may have been their attitude hitherto. This is the period of popular songs such as "God bless you, Tommy Atkins, here's a country's health to you" and "Soldiers of the Queen"—

> And if they ask us how it's done
> And why it is we've always won,
> We'll proudly point to every one
> Of the Soldiers of the Queen.

The sentiment of imperialism, the focusing of that sentiment on the person of the almost legendary Queen, and the popularising of the army were all strengthened during the last years of the reign by the events of the Boer War. This had proved a more serious affair than had been anticipated; perhaps we had forgotten the lessons of Majuba Hill in 1881. But the participation of colonial troops in the campaign, and the Queen's sympathetic and frequently expressed appreciation of the contribution which they were making, played a considerable part in promoting imperial solidarity. There were some people, stigmatised as "pro-Boers", who deplored a war which was being carried on against a nation of farmers who read the Bible and only wanted to be left alone. It was apparently being waged in the interests of big business, represented largely by Jewish capitalists like Barney Barnato and Solly Joel, whose only aim was to exploit the gold and diamond industries. Perhaps it was not so simple as that. But this was not the general feeling and the war afforded an occasion for displays of what is usually regarded as loyalty and patriotism. The little wars of the nineteenth century had been fought by professional redcoats in obscure corners of India or Africa, and had had little repercussion on the ordinary life of the ordinary citizen of this country. But the difficulties and reverses of the Second Boer War, and the example set by the "Colonies", fostered a new attitude. Volunteer regiments were raised and sent to South Africa. Kipling stirred popular sympathy by an egregious piece of doggerel entitled *The Absent-Minded Beggar*; and it was set to equally egregious music by Sir Arthur Sullivan. Aesthetically this production can have added little to the reputation of either the author or the composer, but the song was sung everywhere and was instrumental in raising large sums for the benefit of those whom the troops had "left behind them"—"Pass the hat for your credit's sake, and pay-pay-pay!" There was even a hint of the system of conscription which was destined to be introduced to meet a much more serious situation not many years later—

> Duke's son—cook's son—son of a hundred Kings
> . . . It's all the same today.

Against this background of the Second Boer War three out of my six years at U.C.S. were spent. It was a period when the development of adolescence, and perhaps also the type of education which I was receiving and the influence of J. L. Paton, set me thinking about some of the problems which the adult citizen is called upon to face. By the time that I had reached the Sixth Form I began to be troubled about the morality of war and the implications of imperialism; and it was topics such as these that we discussed from time to time in the school debating society. I was usually on the minority side. All the same, as a London school, we took our share in the excitements of which the Metropolis was the scene. The relief of Mafeking on May 17th, 1900 was the occasion of a mad outburst of public feeling such as was not paralleled even after the end of the First and Second World Wars. Our contribution was to join with a number of students from University College in commandeering a lorry from

Maple's. On the box-seat was set the image of "Phineas", the highlander taking snuff, who in those days belonged to a tobacconist in the Tottenham Court Road,* but who—I believe—has since been adopted as a mascot by the College. Any soldiers or sailors whom we met were placed on the lorry which was dragged by hordes of students and schoolboys down to the Colonial Office in Downing Street where some of the chief excitement was to be found. Another occasion for a display of "patriotic" sentiment was when the City Imperial Volunteers (always known as the "C.I.V.") returned from South Africa and made their triumphal march through the streets of London. We were allowed a half-holiday in order to see the sight; and Paton headed the notice which gave us this permission "C.I.V.—is Romanus sum". All this helped to glamorise the armed forces and to alter the middle-class attitude towards them. The army finally became respectable in 1914 when we were all expected to take an active part in the "war to end war" or "the war to make the world safe for democracy". Some of us who volunteered believed these recruiting slogans to be true; but the years have brought a bitter disillusionment.

All the same, the imperialism of this last phase of the Victorian age blazed up and then as quickly burnt itself out. Fundamentally it was something alien to the British people and not characteristic of it. The Boer War itself, in spite of the settlement which was made and which perhaps did credit to both sides, left a sour taste in the mouth. The conception of a "Commonwealth" which has since developed proved to be more in keeping with British ideas of freedom and co-operation and responsibility; but the world-shattering events which have occurred since the end of Queen Victoria's reign, and their continuing repercussions, have profoundly modified the whole situation. The Empire on which the sun never sets has vanished overnight. We no longer believe with Cecil Rhodes that "we happen to be the best people in the world, with the highest ideals of decency and justice and liberty and peace, and the more of the world we inhabit the better it is

* Later he belonged to Catesby's the furnishers.

for humanity"—or at any rate we do not say so. We leave that for the Americans. Perhaps there is still some room for a Commonwealth of former members of the Empire who retain some sort of English tradition and regard for English institutions; but the outcome is not easy to see.

CHAPTER 14

# Choosing a Career

WHEN I was about 15 we happened to go to tea with a friend's daughter who was training to become a domestic science expert. While she and my stepmother were gossiping I explored her bookcase and found there an elementary textbook of human physiology, written by a certain J. Pilley. I was absolutely fascinated, and being allowed to borrow the volume I read it with avidity and made a précis of it, with careful diagrams, in my "Useful Knowledge Book". In this I had collected such oddments as the Rules of Rugby Football, illustrated particulars of the various styles of architecture, the table of ancient alphabets from the Oxford *Helps to the Study of the Bible*, and other odds and ends. But Pilley's book fired me with a great ambition to be a doctor. It seemed to me then—as indeed it has always seemed since—that medicine is the greatest of all professions. To begin with, it calls for intellectual attainments of a high order; I can even now remember the thrill when I first realised that the doctor's skill lies as much in the diagnosis of a disease as in the treatment of it. But at the same time the doctor must learn to be deft with his hands; and this was even more true in my youth than it is today. Tools have always had a fascination for me, though I never had any opportunity in the school curriculum of learning how to use them; but I should have loved to have that practice in the manipulation of instruments and apparatus which is part of a doctor's business. Again, the high status of medicine as a profession is universally recognised; and above all it affords opportunities for service to the community which appealed to me more and more as I came under the influence of J. L. Paton. It also happened that about this time we joined households with a doctor friend of my father's. He was a bachelor but had hitherto been living with two unmarried sisters. When they set up a separate ménage we went to live in his house and he became a member of our family. This enormously increased my interest in doctoring as a career. I was always talking about medical matters with him and he gave me free run of his books. From time to time we would dissect a rabbit or a bullock's eye; and when the doctor was applying to become police surgeon and was furbishing up his Forensic Medicine, I used to hear him his homework. I remember getting an enormous thrill out of the methods of ascertaining from the appearance of a drowned corpse how long it had been immersed in water. There was also a fascinating chapter on "The Fauna of the Cadaver". But, alas, my hopes of becoming a doctor were doomed to disappointment. It was not a question of finance nor lack of opportunity. But owing to my not very robust physique and the medical history which I had inherited from my mother, it was decided that I must abandon the idea. This decision rankled not only while I was at school, but for many years afterwards; and for long I continued to hope against hope that a way out might be vouchsafed. However, I have come to realise that perhaps the decision may have been a wise one; and at any rate I was fortunate in ultimately finding a career in another profession which, if not so spectacular as medicine, offers equal opportunities of social service.

I had started Latin at the dame-school at the age of 8 or 9 and Greek at Henderson's about two years later; and these two subjects had figured pretty largely in my curriculum ever since. It was therefore decided that I should work for a classical scholarship at Oxford. In this I was encouraged by my father who was a journalist and whose favourite epithets of praise and blame were "literary" and "non-literary". But I am sure that one of the chief reasons for making me specialise in the classics was that there were in those days far more scholarships offered at the older universities in this subject than in any other. This seems a most uneducational reason for cramming a boy into the classical mould regardless of whether he has any special aptitude or liking for Latin and Greek. However, my fate was decided for me and once I got into the Sixth Form the time given to these subjects was increased. I was also in Paton's Greek Testament class and even won the school Greek Testament prize. But I had no particular interest in most of the work which I was required to do, though I never went so far as the Cambridge undergraduate who said that the final syllable should be deleted from the term "Classical Tripos". The books which we had to read seemed so remote from real life. Unseens, to my youthful impatience, appeared to be a kind of missing word competition. Proses were largely a *pastiche* of tags and an exercise in sheer imitation. Once, when I was asked to put a description of King Edward VII's coronation ceremony into Latin, I used the word *incessit* to describe the entry of Queen Alexandra. When Tressler asked me why I had chosen the word I quoted the phrase from the *Æneid* "Vera incessu patuit dea". He was absolutely delighted; but to me the incident seemed simply to illustrate what extraordinary people schoolmasters are—especially those who teach the classics. It was many years afterwards, when I was myself a schoolmaster, that I understood the reason for the praise which I had received.

Although most of the work was a drudgery and I still hankered after medicine, I plodded steadily on. I shall always associate the sixth book of Thucydides and the Syracusan expedition with getting up in the cold and dark winter to do an hour's work before breakfast, sitting in an overcoat with an oil-lamp in a room in which the fire had not yet been lighted. However, my efforts resulted in the award, just before I was 19, of a scholarship at an Oxford college; and there I entered upon a further intensive study of the classics which lasted another four years. But I could not get rid of the medical "bug". The work which I was required to do seemed such a waste of life when I might (as recommended by William Petty) have been "making sceletons and excarnating bowells", and after that have gone on to learn how to diagnose and treat disease. But, as I have already indicated, my whole education, from the day when I first went to the dame-school, had led me to take it for granted that one worked at a prescribed subject, whether one happened to be interested in it or not. But at last there came a day, after I had taken my degree, when I was elected by my College into a senior scholarship which gave me an independence for four more years without any restrictions as to the particular line of study in which I should engage. It was too late to start a medical course, especially as I had never had an elementary grounding in science, but I was at any rate now able to devote myself to subjects which seemed to have some direct relation to the world around me.

The problem of what career I should aim at still remained. Ever since my aspirations to become a doctor had been frustrated I had been toying with the idea of being ordained. By the time that I had arrived in the Sixth Form I was beginning to think seriously about this, but the more I thought the more perplexed I became. One of my chief difficulties concerned the authority of the Bible. I had been brought up to consider this as unquestionably the "lively oracles of God", and the final arbiter of any theological or moral problem. I remember a sermon in which the preacher said "The question for us must always be: Is it in the Bible?" I had also in my earlier teens been made to join a Bible Reading society. One was given a card indicating a few verses to be read each night throughout the year, and this was supposed to have a therapeutic moral value. It was in fact the spiritual equivalent of the daily dose of salts or the sleeping tablet before retiring. But the more I thought about the Bible the more I wondered why faith in the purely theological sense was regarded as a virtue; and I was tempted to regard the "inspired word" as a much over-rated book. To begin with it was not a book at all, but a collection of documents differing widely one from another and containing a large number of variant readings. In some places it reached the sublimest heights of human (or divine) literature; in others it was, to say the very least, unedifying. It included on the one hand records of the life and teachings of our Lord, and on the other the crude folk-lore and blood-stained chronicles of the ancient Israelites who worshipped a tribal God called Jahweh and—like many other nations before and since—regarded themselves as a chosen people. The difficulty was to believe that all this hetero-geneous collection was alike divinely inspired and authoritative in matters of faith. The vast differences of interpretation of this material and the resultant proliferation of sects, all appealing to Biblical inspiration, seemed to weaken the position. In any case who were the people who decided that this particular set of documents was in some special sense the "Word of God", as distinct from all other writings? The fixing of the Canon had been decided by early Christian fathers with whom the Protestant advocates of biblical inspiration would have little in common. And why were some of the Apocalyptic books—e.g. *Ecclesiastes* and *Wisdom*—excluded although they were far more elevating than many parts of the accepted Old Testament? Moreover, the inspired scriptures were not even consistent and could at times be even directly contradictory. In one place the writer congratulates himself on hating the heathen with a "perfect hatred"; in another we are taught to love our enemies. Wine at one time is a mocker and we are warned against looking on it when it is red; at another it rejoices the heart of man and is prescribed for those that be of heavy hearts. Again, David's conduct in the matter of Uriah and Bathsheba seems an utterly base violation of both the sixth and the seventh commandments, and yet we are told that his "heart was perfect with the Lord his God". Solomon, who was regarded as the very impersonation of wisdom, had no less than 700 wives, not to speak of another 300 less regular associates. One is reminded of the old lady who, when informed by her minister of Solomon's exploits in this respect, exclaimed "Lor Sir, what blessed privileges them early Christians 'ad!"

To a Sixth Form schoolboy in his nineteenth year, who had been encouraged to think seriously, problems like this could be very real; and this is probably a stage through which many adolescents go, though nowadays they tend to be more concerned about political, social and international problems. But I had to keep my difficulties to myself. In the environment in which I was living "having doubts" was regarded as almost as horrifying as being dishonest or intemperate or immoral. But I never lost my interest in the English Church—perhaps partly for aesthetic or historical reasons. But even here there were difficulties when one began to think. In spite of the stress laid on the authority of the Bible, every time an orthodox Anglican goes to church he is expected to affirm solemnly that he believes not the inspired scriptures but the Holy Catholic Church—or, in the Nicene version of the Creed, "one Catholic and Apostolic Church". But the creeds themselves, although they were glibly repeated by the congregation, presented difficulties which I never had the opportunity of hearing explained in sermons or elsewhere. Some of the terms which they used (as I afterwards discovered) were the outcome of medieval scholastic theology and it was not easy to put any precise meaning into them. I remember challenging one of my fellow sixth-formers, whose father was a parson and who had definitely made up his mind to enter the Congregational ministry, to explain such phrases as "begotten not made", "being of one substance with the Father", "Who proceedeth from the Father and the Son". There were other more vital issues which were even more difficult to face.

Biblical and theological issues had been debated (though I was hardly aware of it) throughout the nineteenth century—even before the researches of the geologists and the development of prehistory. But in my case the matter was precipitated when I was about 17 by my being awarded a copy of *The Origin of Species* as a school prize. This helped me to realise the implications of the Darwinian Theory of Evolution. My reaction to that was to wonder where exactly the line was drawn between the beasts that perish because they have no souls, and man with his promise of immortality. Somewhere there must have been a progenitor who was a beast and who perished, and a progeny who was a man and had a hope of inheriting eternal life. Unless one could solve this problem it seemed inevitable either that all "beasts"—

even down to bacteria and protoplasm—must have souls, or else that neither beasts nor humans were immortal. When I got to Oxford and became friendly with undergraduates who were reading Theology and aiming at Holy Orders, it became possible to discuss these things more freely and so help to clear one's mind. The result in my case was to decide finally that I did *not* want to be ordained and that I must look elsewhere for a career. In any case there seemed to be disadvantages in having to make up one's mind finally about these fundamental matters at the age of 23. But, as I have said, this did not mean that I wished to sever my connection with the Church into which I had been baptised and confirmed. The latitudinarian variations of the English Church seemed to offer a place for a person with my limitations. A friend of mine was once asked by an importunate "enthusiast" "Are you saved?" To which he replied "No, I'm a member of the Church of England".

As the result of my decision not to aim at Holy Orders I had no idea at the time when my degree course ended what career I should take up. If I had been reading Law or Medicine or Theology or Science or Engineering or almost any other subject the way would have been clear once one had graduated; but the Oxford Honour Classical Moderations and Literae Humaniores Course landed one nowhere in particular. I was extremely fortunate in that my post-graduate scholarship, which lasted for another four years, postponed the necessity of deciding how I was to earn my living. During that time I was able to study subjects in which I was really interested and which I had chosen for myself. I had an opportunity to spend some time in both France and Germany, and also to do a piece of historical research which gave me some experience in the handling of original sources. When I finally decided to become a schoolmaster I was able to profit by all this throughout my teaching career. As it was fated that I could not become a doctor, I have never regretted my decision to embark on this. It was a source of deep and continued satisfaction, and it led on to wider interests than I had imagined when I first took up this work.

The experience which I have had since I finished the classical course which was provided for me at school and during my first four years at Oxford has often made me wonder whether, after all, I might not have been fortunate in the particular kind of specialisation which it afforded. As things were, it is difficult to see what else I could have done. At school my grounding in history had hitherto been of the slightest, and I doubt greatly whether I could have read for a degree in this subject at Oxford— though ultimately I was able to give a good deal of attention to it. Geography had been even more neglected at school, and in any case there were in those days no university honours courses in it. I had certainly made some progress in German and was much attracted by it, but my achievements in French by the time I left school were quite negligible, so that I could hardly have aimed at a modern languages degree. The sciences were absolutely ruled out owing to my lack of initial training. Mathematics interested me, but I was always weak at calculations; so that even if I understood how to do a problem I usually got the working wrong. So if I were to have some form of higher education the solution, upon which both J. L. Paton and my father were agreed, was perhaps the wisest one. I should most certainly not have wished to become a lawyer or a member of the Stock Exchange—two careers at which a number of my schoolfellows were aiming. Nor had I the least inclination towards business; and I knew too much about the inconveniences of a journalist's life to wish to emulate my father. So it is possible that my previous training formed a not unsuitable basis for the work which I was enabled to do during those four post-graduate years and in the years ever since. Even if one accepts all that has been said about the fallacy of "formal training" it remains true that the discipline of studying the classics does at any rate help one to write English, and the content of Literae Humaniores trains one to think.

## CHAPTER 15

# Schooling—Then and Now

THE Victorian system of elementary education had originated from the efforts of two voluntary societies—one founded by the English Church and the other unsectarian. From 1833 onwards they received some aid in the form of an annual government grant; and from 1862 the amount of this had been assessed not only on the attendance of pupils, but also on the results of an examination which they were required to undergo and which was conducted by a government inspector. This was the system known as "payment by results", and though it was modified as time went on it did not completely disappear until the end of the century. As the voluntary societies were incapable of providing an adequate system of popular education, the Act of 1870 gave us such a system by setting up school boards, the function of which was to "fill up gaps", i.e. to provide elementary education where there was an insufficient supply of voluntary schools. The board schools, like the voluntary schools, were eligible for government grant; but, unlike them, they also received rate aid. Thus was introduced the "dual system"; and though the school boards disappeared in 1902 the duality, in a modified form, remains.

Practically all my schooldays were spent during the school-board period, though—as I have already indicated—I belonged to a different educational stream which took no part in these things. In the year before I left school to go up to Oxford the 1902 Education Act was passed. The only interest that it had for me was that it gave rise to the movement known as "passive

resistance". The Act brought into being a state system of secondary schools and extended government aid to many old grammar
schools which had hitherto been independent, though some had
endowments. But it also made rate aid available to the voluntary
schools, most of which were provided by the Church of England,
and a respectable minority by the Roman Catholics. A section of
the nonconformist community led by a certain Dr. Clifford, who
was minister of a chapel at Westbourne Park, refused to pay the
school rate and was prepared to suffer distraint of goods in con-
sequence. The "Nonconformist Conscience" was belauded or
derided, according to one's point of view; but among my dissenting relatives Dr. Clifford was regarded almost in the light of
an early Christian martyr. To an impartial observer it might have
seemed illogical that a religious group which since 1833 had been
paying taxes, out of which annual grants had been made to the
voluntary schools, should in 1902 violently and conscientiously
object to a subsidy for such schools in the form of rates. The
controversy caused much excitement at the time, and was even
discussed in the School Debating Society; but the significance of
the 1902 Act was not realised by myself—nor, I suspect, by many
other people—until long afterwards.

The Act provided us at last with something like a national
system of education. But the two "streams", typified by Disraeli's
"Two Nations", still existed. In 1907 a scheme was introduced
for easing this situation and facilitating the access to secondary
education for promising children from elementary schools. All
grant-aided schools (which did not, of course, include independent
schools of any kind) were now to admit, as free-place scholars, a
percentage of pupils who had spent at least two years at an
elementary school; the rest still paid fees. This provision caused
some uneasiness among the more class-conscious of the parents
of this latter group. But there was an increasing body of opinion
which believed that, even if there were now channels cut between
the "elementary" and "secondary" streams, we should still
never have a satisfactory system of national education until there
was only one stream. The idea of "elementary" and "secondary"

as *types* of education should be discarded. Their place should be taken by a system of primary and secondary education end on to one another, and the term "elementary" should be abolished. The scope of secondary education should be widened so as to include not only schools with an academic type of curriculum, like that of the old grammar schools, but also those which gave courses of a more technical or realistic nature. These matters were dealt with by several committees of experts, and their *Reports* are landmarks in the educational history of the last three decades. But it was not until the Act of 1944 that a system of national education in successive stages was fully realised. The outstanding problems which it has left to us are how to determine the organisation of the different varieties of secondary education which are provided, and the method by which primary school children are to be allocated to the various types of secondary school or course.

One of the most debated attempts to deal with this situation is provided by the comprehensive school. This includes the various types of secondary education in the same institution, and to it children living in a given area are drafted without a selection test. But if justice is to be done alike to the quick learners and the slow learners and the different kinds of ability are to be catered for, there must be "streams" and special courses even in the comprehensive school, and some means must be devised for allocating children to them. Unfortunately the comprehensive principle is not always argued on purely educational grounds, and political or theoretical presumptions may tend to decide the matter. Where this involves merging an existing grammar school, which may have a long history and a strong community feeling and vigorous life, in an unwieldy new institution where it will lose its identity, there is sure to be opposition from certain quarters. Parents, for example, may feel uneasy about so radical a change. Teachers whose training and whole experience have been in grammar school work, may find themselves—without even having been consulted—transferred to an entirely different kind of environment with which they may not be in sympathy.

Another group, which is affected but which normally is disregarded completely, is the old pupils who maintain their loyalty to their school and run flourishing "Old ... ians'" Societies. They tend not unnaturally to deprecate strongly the merging of their old school in a huge composite type of institution where its history and traditions and personality will be lost. The comprehensive experiment is an interesting one and educationally well worth trying; but the proper place for making it would seem to be the new housing estates where there would be no fear of interference with existing secondary schools. In any case it is surely unwise to take drastic and far-reaching decisions on grounds simply of theoretical principle or administrative convenience.

People in Parliament and outside sometimes speak as if the state system of education was the whole of the picture. But even under modern conditions the independent schools play an important part in national education. In some quarters it is felt to be unduly important. Thus, in spite of the 1944 Act, there are still two parallel streams—the free primary–secondary state system, and the independent preparatory–public school system in which fees (sometimes very heavy ones) are paid. Two government committees—those presided over by Lord Fleming (1944) and by Sir John Newsom (1968)—have been appointed to see whether some contact could be made between the two systems on the lines of the 1907 "free-place" scheme described above. It can hardly be said that their recommendations have so far had much effect.

There is no doubt whatever that the state system has undergone a spectacular transformation since the beginning of the present century, and that the pace has increased under the impetus provided by two world wars. It is possible that the developments in the "independent" system—the one in which I was educated—have been less fundamental; and one reason for that may be that this system had a flying start and that, in some respects, or in some cases, it retains its lead. For example, I look back to the kindergarten which I attended from 1889 to 1891. As I have already said, its techniques compared quite favourably with those of the modern infant school. Songs, games, dancing, miming, handwork—activities of all kinds—played a large part in the curriculum. Those of us who stayed to dinner at school were also taught table manners and made to wash our hands and look after ourselves. But we had one outstanding advantage which even the most modern infant school too rarely possesses— the advantage of small classes. This was also the case at the "School for the Sons of Gentlemen", at Henderson's, and even to some extent at U.C.S. At the kindergarten there were rarely more than twelve or fifteen pupils in a group. A short time before these lines were written I saw two lessons given in an infants' school in a large and prosperous manufacturing town in the north of England. In one class there were fifty-one children and in the other fifty-three. In both cases they were crammed into a class-room so small that it was impossible even to preserve proper gangways. If a child at the back wished to go out during a lesson it was possible to do so only by climbing over chairs and desks occupied by other members of the class. Of course, any kind of educational "activity" was out of the question. When I see some of the splendid new school buildings which are the pride of local Education Authorities and are shown by chief education officers to interested visitors from abroad, I wish that the butter could be spread more evenly over the bread. The advantages provided even by the best-equipped schools tend inevitably to be neutralised so long as classes—especially classes of very young children—are so large that it is practically impossible for the teacher to give them adequate attention as individuals. The former Ministry of Education, in its *School Grant Regulations*, prescribed a class maximum of forty pupils for all but the most senior children in a primary school, and thirty pupils in a secondary school. These numbers—as the example quoted above shows—are often exceeded in practice. But there seems no sound educational reason why the maximum for the primary school should be higher than that for the secondary school. It is certainly most desirable that as many as possible of our youngsters should get their first impressions of school in a bright and airy building, set in pleasant and open surroundings. But even more important is a class small enough to enable the teacher to maintain close contact with, and interest in, each individual member of it. This is true at any stage. We ought to give our teachers the best possible conditions under which to do their job —not, of course, primarily for their benefit, but for that of the children. If a choice had to be made, reducing the size of classes should have the priority. Vita-glass windows, television equipment, grand pianos and swimming-baths are excellent things to have; but ultimately an efficient extra teacher on the staff is better. The difficulty nowadays is to find him (or her).

The development of educational theory during the past half-century has implied a criticism both of curriculum and of methods of instruction. In the elementary schools of late Victorian times— even at the "School for the Sons of Gentlemen", at Henderson's and at U.C.S.—the aim was largely to impart a quantity of information which, it was thought, would at some time prove useful, or, at any rate, would provide "mental training". The methods, therefore, of imparting this knowledge relied largely on drill and memorisation, though what was learnt was not always understood. In the contemporary board and voluntary schools the classes were usually so large that it was quite impossible to deal with pupils as individuals or to grade them properly. The same information had to be dished out to everyone alike and attention was enforced by strict discipline. But these conditions were to some extent mitigated in the schools which I attended because, as I have said, all of them had smaller classes than were usual in the elementary schools. It may also be claimed, perhaps, that rote methods, however "uneducational" they may be (and that is not disputed), did at any rate encourage habits of hard work. But the last fifty years have seen a swing of the educational pendulum from one extreme to the other. The learning by heart of fact knowledge tends to be discarded as being an unnecessary burden on the mind and as discouraging reasoning. The shift of interest from the subject taught to the pupil himself—a fundamentally important reform—is taken to imply that the child should follow his own interests and choose his own experiences. Emphasis is no longer laid on passive reception, but on active "self-expression". An outward and visible sign of this has been the replacement in primary schools of fixed desks or benches by movable tables and chairs, with a consequent relaxation of strict class-discipline. Even if this movement has been handicapped in many instances by failure to reduce the size of classes, the underlying principles are everywhere accepted. At the same time it is beginning to be realised that "activities" are not necessarily valuable in themselves and that "self-realisation" is meaningless unless the self has something worth while to express. But if the present shortage of teachers persists or worsens, and more and more recourse has to be had to expedients such as the mechanical devices which provide or check sheer information, we may run the danger of being back in the position of the nineteenth-century elementary schools.

A serious criticism of the education which I received, and which I suspect was less applicable to the contemporary state schools, was the neglect of physical and aesthetic education. Even at the kindergarten, though there was plenty of games, there was no opportunity, so far as I can remember, for activities out-of-doors. At my next school there was no provision whatever for any kind of physical education. At Henderson's we played organised games, but there was no form of gymnastics or drill or exercises of that kind. The same is true of U.C.S. There we certainly had a first-class gymnasium and I spent much of my out-of-class time there. But the instruction which we received was an "extra", and not part of the normal curriculum. Only a small proportion of the pupils, therefore, benefited from it. Even the organised games on the school field at Neasden were not compulsory, though normally the consulting master would exert pressure on a boy who wanted to contract out, unless he had good reason for so doing. The concept of "total education" which is concerned with the body, as well as with the mind and spirit, is a powerful and significant development in modern educational theory; and the playing of organised games is only one element in it.

Again, it was quite usual to make no provision for any form of aesthetic education in the curriculum of the independent school, or at any rate to teach it out of ordinary school hours and to charge an extra fee for it. At no time after leaving the kindergarten was I given any instruction in singing, though (as I have explained) we had voluntary, out-of-school community singing at U.C.S. The piano lessons at the "School for the Sons of Gentlemen" were, I think, not typical of this kind of school; and in any case there was no attempt to interest us in *music*, as such. The great opportunities, by which I was fortunate enough to profit, came to me entirely from agencies quite outside the school—from my home and from private lessons. In the same way there was little or no encouragement inside the ordinary school curriculum for artistic development; and such teaching as there was tended to be formal and to give little scope for imagination. I remember that in one of the form-rooms at U.C.S. there was a large picture of Lord Leighton—a distinguished Old Gower who had become President of the Royal Academy; but the school could certainly take no credit for having contributed to his education as an artist.

But perhaps the most serious lacuna in the education which I received, both at school and at the university, was that it included no instruction whatever in science. I have tried since to fill the gap, as best I can, by private reading; but when one is immersed in the duties of adult life opportunities for repairing one's educational deficiencies are limited. In any case desultory reading is no substitute for the training which a properly designed science course can provide. I can find much of fascinating interest in—let us say—the *Penguin Science News* or the *New Biology*; but at the same time a great deal is quite unintelligible, or I can only guess at what it means, simply because of my lack of a grounding in scientific knowledge. It seems absurd that one who has survived into the technological age should be handicapped in this way. It can surely be taken as a real advance made during the past half-century or so that a lop-sided education of this kind would be quite impossible today. The danger now is that, if we are not careful, there may be a lop-sidedness in the other direction.

Perhaps the most marked influence which the independent schools have exerted has been by the example which they have set of corporate life and extra-curricular activities. The movement had started at least as early as the days of Thomas Arnold, who was Headmaster of Rugby from 1828 to 1842; but it spread and affected the old grammar schools, many of which became grant-earning secondary schools after 1902. With the development of the national system of education the tradition has become common to all types of schools. Today secondary modern—even primary—schools have as vivid and many-sided a school-life as any other kind of day school; and they are served as devotedly by their teachers as schools which have inherited an older tradition. They have their prefects and school uniform and "colours", which are outward and visible signs of their corporate life. In my youth such things were utterly unknown in "elementary" schools, and we should have bitterly resented it if the board schools had copied us in these respects. But since those days the tradition which they typify has filtered through from the public schools and has been adapted to the conditions of a day school which draws its pupils from homes in which the significance of such practices is not always even yet fully appreciated.

In our educational world there are still two nations—that of the fee-paying independent school and that of the free primary-secondary state school. As Sir Cyril Norwood, who was for eight years Headmaster of Harrow, has said: "It is impossible to hope that the classes of this country will ever be united in spirit unless their members cease to be educated in two separate systems of schools, one of which is counted as definitely inferior to the other."* We have still a long way to go before we achieve complete "equality of opportunity" or "parity of status"; but the two systems have drawn closer together than they were in my youth. The curriculum, for example, in the state secondary

* "The Crisis in Education", in the *Spectator* of Feb. 9th, 1940.

grammar schools is approximately the same as that in the public schools; they both take the same public examinations, and the former make as good a show as the latter in the competition for university places and entrance scholarships. The primary schools now draw their pupils from a wide range of social classes, though the secondary modern school still tends—quite unjustly—to be handicapped by the bad old "elementary" tradition of the "senior school". But the whole outlook on school work and life has changed, and in this respect there is far less difference between the two streams than there used to be. The reason why they persist, therefore, is obviously not an *educational* one. In this country educational developments may ultimately affect social progress, but it is equally true that our educational system is still largely determined by our social set-up. It is possible to claim that a definition of democracy, which includes a measure of individual freedom, should imply the right to buy a particular form of education for one's children if one does not wish them to have that which is provided free by the State. But there are also some grounds for the criticism that the independent schools have produced a clique which secures for itself an unduly large share in the control of the country's affairs and that it is thus at once a cause and an effect of social stratification. This criticism is strongly felt in some quarters and it is responsible for the attacks which from time to time are made on the public-school system. It accounts also for the appointment of the Fleming Committee and the Newsom Commission to which reference has already been made.

CHAPTER 16

# A Final Retrospect

IN MY Introduction and from time to time in subsequent chapters
I have stressed the enormous change which has come over society
since the last period of Queen Victoria's reign, and how in particular educative influences affecting young people have altered
within the space of a single lifetime—my own. I want now to
amplify this topic a little and look back on the experience of my
childhood and adolescence, and then consider the conditions
under which young people now live. The changes to which I
have referred are usually thought of in terms of scientific advance
and social "security". As I have indicated, there may be another
side to this and it may, in some measure at any rate, be a specious
kind of progress. For example, it is doubtless a great achievement
to land a human being on the moon, but one is tempted to
wonder what is the real purpose and significance of such exploits.
They may be quite literally what Stephen Leacock has called "the
larger lunacy". We are not likely to colonise our satellite with
our surplus population, or to raise food or secure raw materials
from it to supply the needs of our own planet. One always has
the uneasy suspicion that the ultimate motive behind these
attempts is a military one, and that those who now hold the
power to destroy human civilisation at the press of a button may
be devising yet more subtle and effective methods of achieving
this end. It is noticeable that the "cosmonauts" or "astronauts",
as they are called, are almost always military officers. It seems

unlikely that nations like America and Russia would spend untold sums on attempts of this kind simply and solely for the sake of pure unbiased scientific research.

Great as have been the material developments in our world owing to these scientific advances, the changes in the moral attitudes and norms of the middle-class society in which I was brought up have been hardly less striking. Values and standards which were then uncritically accepted are now challenged or disregarded. The result has been to put a strain on young people which we were not called upon to endure. In my youth religious influences, even if they were very often the outcome of un-questioning habit, were very real—particularly perhaps in the type of middle-class environment in which I grew up. At the same time, we were not subjected to the irresponsible barrage of sensationalism which today is exerted by the popular press and by many forms of popular entertainment. The private life of film-stars, the activities of gangsters and criminals, the exploita-tion of vice and of scandals involving well-known figures in society, the antics of "pop" singers and drug addicts and their fanatical following—these and similar trivia were not held up year in and year out as objects of interest and even admiration; and we were not continually indoctrinated with the theory that the only things in life that really matter are sex, money and entertainment.

Of course it was possible, or even habitual, to be narrow-minded. One's speech habits were carefully supervised. "Swearing" was associated with "working men" and regarded as not merely definitely sinful, but (what was almost worse) "un-gentlemanly". It was only the "lower classes" who said "bloody", or "damn" or used similar wicked expressions. I remember, for example, that in our "pokey villa" days we had only one maid-servant and she was a London-bred damsel named Kate. On one occasion for some reason her younger sister came to spend a few days with her. This girl, aged about 14, created a tremendous sensation by saying to me, as I was sitting on the floor, "Get up, you devil". There was an improving verse which ran

Naughty little cuss words,
"Bother", "dash", and "blow",
Lead you on to wuss words
And send you down below.

All the same it was rather fun to pretend to be a member of the class which was privileged to make use of these verbal safety-valves. One used to invent artificial expletives—e.g. "Oh, blunge it", or "I'll be grabbled if I do."

But it is not only with regard to the wickedness of "swearing" that middle-class social attitudes have changed. Words are now bandied about and freely used in the popular press which in my young days were utterly taboo in polite society and would probably be used only in a technical or scientific treatise—expressions like "contraception" or "homosexuality". The obscene jokes, which boys think funny, in my school days dealt with the natural functions of micturition and defaecation rather than with sexual matters. The stage of dirty sex-jokes came somewhat later. But sex was always regarded as something furtive and underhand. We now seem to have gone to the other extreme. In the late Victorian days modesty was still generally regarded as a female virtue. Sex problems must always present difficulties for adolescents, but the modern throwing over of restraints and the recent development of the cult of the young woman must have had considerable impact on our young people of both sexes. In my youth the bookstalls were not covered with garish pictures of glamorous and seductive females in various stages of undress, and the beach at the seaside in the summer did not exhibit lines of sunbathing young women whose main object seems to be to expose as much of themselves as they dare. Again, the use of cosmetics and other aids to beauty (at any rate if it was at all obvious) was considered to be vulgar and not respectable. If one saw a woman who was in the least "made up", the proper course was to give an appropriate shudder and pass by on the other side. The "half angel, half idiot" conception still had some vigour, in spite of periodic agitations for "women's rights". As Frederick Harrison said in the early 1890's: "To keep the family

true, refined, affectionate, faithful, is the woman's task—a task
that needs the entire energies and life of a woman; and to mix up
this sacred duty with the grosser occupation of politics and trade
is to unfit her for it." How the world has changed since the
beginning of the present century! Yet the old "Square", when he
sees a steatopygous young woman clad in tightly fitting trousers
or a "miniskirt", and reminding one of the Ancient Mariner's
Nightmare Life-in-Death—

> Her lips were red, her looks were free,
> Her locks were yellow as gold—

cannot help feeling that in spite of bustles and tight-lacing, the
female sex really did things better in those by-gone days, and that
dignity and refinement (unlike "caparisons") do become a young
woman.

There is, however, a much more serious, significant and permanent side to all this, and that is the great development which
has been effected since the latter years of the nineteenth century in
the education of girls and the part which women play in society.
Throughout the century a good deal of thought had been given
to problems of national education, and the system set up in 1870
applied, of course, to girls as much as to boys. By 1880 compulsory
schooling for both sexes from the age of 5 up to at least the age of
10 had been introduced. But, as has been indicated, to send a
child from a middle-class family to an "elementary" school, run
by a school board or a voluntary agency, would have been
regarded as a serious loss of caste; and the daughters of such
families would normally be found in the "independent" stream.
The majority of such girls attended private establishments—at the
primary stage co-educational kindergartens and then female
equivalents of the Henderson preparatory school type. They
would proceed to ladies' seminaries up to the age of 16 or 18.
These latter were privately owned and they laid considerable
stress on accomplishments. All this is not to say that there were not
already in existence a growing number of grammar schools for
girls on much the same lines as those available for boys. For

example, Miss Buss's North London Collegiate School, although it started as a private concern in 1850, was transferred to a body of trustees in 1871. The Girls' Public Day School Trust dates from 1872. Miss Beale's Cheltenham Ladies' College, founded in 1853, was a boarding-school run on public school lines. When the Taunton Commission between 1864 and 1868 investigated "secondary" schools it recommended the increased provision of such establishments for girls, and as a result a number of old endowed schools for boys opened sister schools on the same foundation. All this did not mean that in the latter part of last century there were equal facilities for middle-class girls to get to a grammar school, such as would be regarded as socially befitting them. It was not really until the Education Act of 1902 made the provision of secondary as well as elementary education a duty of county and county borough councils that a spate of new "L.E.A." grammar schools came into existence.

Looking back then to the 1880's and 1890's, I find it is surprising how comparatively few of the girls of my own age, who were members of my family or daughters of our friends, went to a school which would be a female equivalent of U.C.S., or even of any kind of modern grammar school for girls. They were apparently still being educated—possibly in many cases quite efficiently—in private schools of the type to which reference has been made. It was no uncommon sight to see such a school out for its daily exercise. The girls walked two and two, the shorter ones in front and the taller ones behind. An assistant mistress led the way and the buxom and imposing head-mistress closed the procession. The whole imposing cavalcade was called a "crocodile".

It is also noteworthy how few of my female contemporaries went on to any form of higher education. Such facilities certainly existed. University colleges and courses had gradually been made available to women from at least the middle of the nineteenth century, though it was not until the latter part of it that some universities eventually opened their degrees to them. I do not know where their candidates came from—possibly for the most part from the pioneer grammar or public schools for girls to which I have referred; but I do know that very few of the girls in my middle-class entourage availed themselves of such opportunities. I certainly had an aunt (only seven years older than myself) who studied at the Royal Academy of Music, but she never taught music or used it professionally. Vera Brittain when discussing, in a book published in 1928,* the problem of women's employment, says of the contemporary girl: "Sometimes—though fortunately for herself less frequently than the well-to-do girl of fifteen years ago—she will choose, if she can afford it, a life of idleness and futility rather than face the inquiries and investigations which must be made before she can find her way into an absorbing occupation." If that could be said in reference to the year 1913, it was much more the case in the last two decades of the nineteenth century.

Again, although a Technical Instruction Act of 1889 gave an impetus to the provision of practical courses of many kinds, as far as girls were concerned—as Alice Zimmern shows†—they tended to concentrate on domestic arts such as cooking, needlework, dress cutting and making, laundry-work and housewifery. Shorthand, typing and the secretarial arts took a subordinate place. But I think attendance at such courses would be to some extent, at any rate, confined to girls from the "elementary" stream. For them it was regarded as usual to get a job upon leaving school at 12 or 13—in domestic work or a shop or a factory or on a farm. But the middle-class girl, who stayed on at school till 18, filled in the time until she got married; in fact it was not unknown for a girl—like the three little maids in the *Mikado*—to get married almost immediately upon leaving school. The aunt, at whose wedding I acted as a page, was married on her eighteenth birthday. Yet, remembering what type of persons these girls of my young days were, I cannot believe that, even if they did not get a job, they lived lives of "idleness and futility". Even though maid-servants were available, they doubtless helped with the housekeeping or busied themselves with church work.

* *Women's Work in Modern England*, p. 2.
† *The Renaissance of Girls' Education*, chap. IX.

In country areas it was their part to look after the poor and needy members of their community. They played the piano and painted; they made collections of shells or dried flowers—I possess an album of preserved specimens of ferns made by a female relative some time in the 1880's. If owing to *res angusta domi* it was really necessary for a middle-class young woman to get a job, she probably became a governess, like those who gave me my first lessons, or else a "companion", like the lady who became my stepmother. The tradition had not yet really been broken.

As far as games and physical activities for girls were concerned, in the private schools the "crocodile" walk was often the only official form of exercise provided, though ball games of a not too strenuous type were usually allowed and were played in the back garden of the school premises. Further opportunities were afforded in schools modelled more definitely on boys' grammar schools, though even Miss Buss in 1880 expressed the opinion that only "rough girls" would take part in games. However, the example of the boys' grammar or public school gradually led to the provision of facilities for hockey or cricket or net-ball—and increasingly so after the turn of the century. In my childhood and youth, tennis was popular with the female sex; but the modern schoolgirl or young lady would regard it contemptuously as "pat ball". Women played it in long dresses reaching right down to the ankles and wearing hats and they served underhand. Men certainly had flannels, but they often wore knickers and black stockings instead of long duck trousers. Many houses, which had a garden large enough, sported a grass tennis-court. We had one at Thornton Heath and I earned many a three-pence by acting as "ball boy". Croquet, which had been very popular in the 1860's and 1870's was still played by young females and it ensured that they did not overdo the physical exertion. Archery also was patronised. With the development of the non-private education of girls a system of physical training called "calisthenics" was introduced. In Foster Watson's *Encyclopaedia and Dictionary of Education*,* published as late as 1921, it says "the

* Vol. I, p. 254.

physique of the town-bred, middle-class girl is often so poor and her curriculum so overcrowded that hockey and cricket are sometimes found to be too strenuous". It therefore recommends instead "short games of tennis" and says that "calisthenics are rather better placed" and should be taught in a gymnasium and with special apparatus. The aim of calisthenic exercises was to impart grace of movement and elegance of deportment, and not merely to promote health and physical strength. Dancing, of course, always formed part of the girls' school curriculum, but largely because of its social implications. More formal drill with Indian clubs or dumb-bells sometimes found a place; and, as we have seen, the turn of the century saw a great development in cycling for women, especially after the introduction of the pneumatic tyre. I think it was a little time, however, before the practice spread downwards to schoolgirls.

The opening of the universities and professions to women and the increase of facilities for the higher education of girls, which marked the latter decades of the nineteenth century, were linked with a more general demand for a public realisation of the part which women should play in the social and political life of the country. The movement for their enfranchisement had been gathering momentum all through the century. J. S. Mill's *Subjection of Women* dates from 1869. In 1870 women were allowed a vote for school boards and were eligible for membership of them. From 1888 onwards they could vote for county councils and even be elected as a councillor or a mayor. But the parliamentary franchise was still denied to them, and by the time of my schooldays "Votes for Women" had become a hotly debated political issue. The militant activities of the Women's Social and Political Union, founded in 1903, familiarised the public with the sort of demonstration which has since become the stock-in-trade of those who have a cause to advocate. Window smashing, arson and hunger strikes certainly drew attention to the claims of the suffragettes; but there were many people who argued that if the militant advocates of female suffrage backed up their cause by such acts of violence it proved that women were not fit to be entrusted with political responsibility, and even those who did not go as far as this tended to take the rather sentimental view expressed by Frederick Harrison.* A series of lists published as late as 1910–11 included among "prominent anti-suffragists" such well-known figures as Lord Curzon of Kedleston, Lord Milner, Joseph Chamberlain, Rudyard Kipling, Professor A. V. Dicey and the actress Phyllis Broughton.

The more violent aspects of the Votes for Women campaign came after I had left school, but even when I was at U.C.S. the issue was a very live one. I remember the subject being discussed in the debating society in my last year there. I proposed the motion that "Women should be given the vote", but it was lost, according to a contemporary report in the *Gower*, by 10 votes to 18. It was about the same time that I attended a women's suffrage meeting in Suburbia. There was a good deal of heckling and certain amount of rowdyism, and finally a stink-bomb was let off which had the effect of closing the proceedings. However, the cause at last was won during the 1914–18 war. Then women took over the work done by men not only in manual occupations, but in businesses, banks, public offices and many other walks of life. The contribution which they made to the war effort and to maintaining the life of the nation was realised and appreciated, and there no longer seemed any serious reason why women who had shared equal duties and responsibilities with men should not also share an equal citizenship. So at last in February 1918 women got the vote, and the large female contingent of workers in all branches of industry, commerce and the professions has not only remained with us, but has vastly increased ever since. The change in this respect since Victoria's latter days has to be lived through to be adequately realised.

Yet another revolution has been seen in the development of the labour movement and of the power of trade unions. My father and grandfather regarded themselves as advanced liberals, but they certainly did not advocate the classless society. For them "socialism" was almost as much a bugbear as anarchism or

* See pp. 152–3.

Marxism. They were politically interested in such topics as Home Rule for Ireland, Disestablishment and the other items of Mr. Gladstone's programme, and it was in such causes that they tried to interest me as I grew older. But a portent of things to come was symbolised by my grandfather's friend, John Burns. He was a forerunner of the labour movement and one of the protagonists of the Independent Labour Party which was founded in 1893. Strikes in those days were by no means unknown. Miners, cotton operatives, engineers and many other industrial workers took part in such demonstrations during the 1890's and much distress and dislocation were caused from time to time. Burns himself was a member of the Amalgamated Society of Engineers, and he took a leading part in the great dock strike of 1889 which held up the trade of the Port of London for ten weeks. But these things did not seem to have much direct impact on the ordinary middle-class citizen. The country did not suffer a continual wave of strikes, whether "official" or "unofficial", which threaten the basis of the national economy and paralyse industry. Perhaps the situation was steadied by stable prices. Society was not subjected to a continual rise in the cost of living which engenders repeated demands for wage increments from all sorts of quarters. In my youth a pound was worth a pound from one year's end to the next and one knew where one was. Moreover, it was a gold sovereign with the Queen's head on one side and St. George and the dragon on the other. The only paper money was the £5 note or higher denominations. Our present £1 and 10/- notes date from the time of the First World War. Moreover, foreign exchanges also remained steady. One knew, for example, that a franc would always be worth $9\frac{1}{2}d$. and coinage among the European countries which belonged to the "Latin Union" was interchangeable.

Taking a final look back at the world of my childhood and youth I can gratefully acknowledge that elements of real progress have been achieved since those late Victorian days in education and the range of knowledge, in standards of health and comfort, in social welfare and justice, in the blurring of class distinctions.

But at the same time, as I have already indicated, there are influences at work in modern society which have enormously increased the task of education in both the narrow and wider sense, because instead of co-operating with it they often militate against it. For example, the school encourages habits of self-restraint and high standards of personal behaviour, of service and unselfishness and responsibility. It seeks to foster worth-while intellectual and aesthetic interests. But too often powerful outside influences tend to counteract its efforts and there is a disharmony between the two agencies. I recently attended an educational conference which was addressed by the headmistress of a very well-known girls' public school. She had just been visiting Russia and she gave us a well-balanced and impartial account of her impressions of its educational system. When she had finished a teacher who was sitting next to me commented: "Well, I should simply hate to live under a communist régime, but it is at any rate consistent as between school and society." What he obviously meant was that in Russia—and it may be true of some non-communist countries too—the same set of values (largely political ones, of course) are inculcated in the school and in the regimented society outside; so that there is no—or very little—contradiction between them. Is it a drawback to the enjoyment of greater freedom in this country that we cannot secure some measure of that "consistence"?

As an illustration of our greater consistence in this respect in my youthful days one can take the fact that we were not conscious of any gap or opposition or lack of sympathy between our own generation and the previous one. We were usually content to accept without question or resentment the norms inculcated by our parents and teachers and prescribed by the middle-class society in which we were growing up. Our world had not yet been shattered by wars and fundamentally divisive political movements. Young people were not tempted to protest violently or otherwise against the mess which their progenitors all the world over had made of things.

I realise the narrowness and extreme class-consciousness of my

Victorian education, but I believe that it had valuable characteristics which might still be imitated with profit—not least its
emphasis on the cultivation of habits of hard work. Even the
narrowness and class-consciousness at any rate gave one standards
of behaviour and responsibility which were a steadying influence
especially during the period of adolescence. But nothing can
recapture the background against which our schooling was set
and which provided our "cosmic" education. We have moved
irrevocably to an age which, for better or worse, seems to have
little in common with that of my Victorian youth. Perhaps one
need not be simply a prejudiced *laudator temporis acti* to feel
nostalgic and to be thankful that one is not destined to spend
one's life in the brave new world which applied science is preparing for us and which seems so often to be hailed as the
millenium. Improved standards of living should have implied
the raising of ethical standards, as well as of material and intellectual ones. Our problem today, as Basil Willey has said,* is
"how to retain the benefits of modern knowledge and modern
enlightenment without sacrificing the values of an older and less
self-conscious order". We live in an age of transition at an ever-
increasing pace; but even so we can still have faith and hope that
before it is too late mankind will realise that the greatest of these
three is charity—ά γαπ ή—love.

* *Ideas and Beliefs of the Victorians*, p. 43.